LISA HELEN GRAY
EVAN

A CARTERS BROTHER NOVEL BOOK 3.5

EVAN

ONE

EVAN

FINDING OUT YOUR MOM isn't your mom and that your biological mom was killed by the woman who pretended to be your mother for twenty-eight years, really fucking sucks.

I always knew I was adopted. I remembered an old couple before moving in with my dad. They were loving and kind and nothing like the mother I grew up with. I remember always thinking, 'take me back to them'. It wasn't until they let me near my sister that I knew I needed to stay. Someone had to protect her.

I failed.

In so many ways.

Not only from my mother, but from the evil outside the four walls we lived in. When I failed to protect her from one of the gangs from around our town I knew I had to step up. I needed to make the right choices instead of always making the wrong ones.

It's what brought me to now.

"Are you sure we can't change your mind to stay?" my now old boss, William, asks me. He's just pissed he doesn't have anyone my age on his force team now to go undercover. After the last nine years of doing it and nearly losing my sister, then finding out she was pregnant and so on, I need to get a life. In the literal sense too. I want what she has. She's getting married soon and has a baby. I want that. No, I need that in my life. I'm not saying I'm ready for kids, I'm nowhere near ready, but the getting married part, settling down, that I do want. I'm ready.

"No, Sir. I need to do this," I tell him for the tenth time this afternoon. I'd just finished packing my stuff up from my office when I got called into his. He's been at me for a month since I handed in my notice to stay on. I had to finish off the few cases I had left open before I could leave. It wasn't required of me, but I'd feel like I left the job undone if I left them open.

"Well, I'm sad to see you go, but, Son, if you ever, and I mean, ever, want to come back to the job, there will always be a job here waiting for you."

"Thank you, Sir, but I'm invested in the new business."

"Ah, the security bodyguard gig."

I laugh. He doesn't get it. It's not just about security for the rich and famous or that I'll be installing security systems, it's the fact it's something I love to do. I've always wanted to get in this side of work. Yeah, I'll still have the odd occasional job where I'll most likely have to go spy on someone's spouse cheating, but it's all in good faith. One day I'll get the business to a place where it needs. As it is we're doing better than most companies like us do in the first few months of starting. We've got some pretty high paying clients, some security instalments lined up and a few jobs here and there.

"Yeah. Look, I need to get going, but I'll see you tonight?" I ask picking up my box of belongings.

"Will you?" he asks looking confused. The guy couldn't hide a secret if it was worth his life. How he managed to get this job is a bloody mystery.

"I heard you telling the boys you'll meet us at the Cavan at ten," I tell him dryly.

"Fuck! Don't let on that you know," he shrugs, rubbing his large hands down his face. The guy really needs to exercise more.

"See you later," I laugh, walking out. Everyone looks up from their desks, giving me chin lifts. I extend one back until I get to the front desk and my face falls. This is the part of the job I'll never miss. I fucking hate walking in and seeing her face every day.

"Evan," she coos, smirking. "We're going to miss you around here. How about we get together tonight and give you a proper send off? We don't have anything standing between us anymore."

I cringe. The woman is a life-size Barbie doll and I'm not fucking kidding. In fact, she looks more plastic than a Barbie.

"Yeah, I also don't have to worry about losing my job now either, so I can say what I like. Fuck off and pester someone else to get your rocks off." I leave her standing at her desk with her mouth hanging wide open. Though, I'm pretty sure she's used to her mouth being open like that. I wouldn't put it past her if she had every STD known to mankind. She's the definition of the word 'slut'.

BACK AT MY PLACE IT isn't much better than my time with Sally on the front desk. Lexi is waiting and she's brought her date with her.

Ever since my sister's kidnapping the woman has changed. I thought we were getting close, you know, close to becoming something more than friends. But when I tried to kiss her she backed off and told me she was dating, that she was seeing someone.

Talk about kick a man when he's down.

I never realised it until then that my feelings for Lexi came only from my need to settle down. And because I believed Lexi was the easiest person to do that with. Everything with her seemed easy. I just never really looked deep enough. Sometimes the way she looked at me made me wonder if she saw me as more than a friend. All the signs were there. She was constantly calling me, talking to me until early hours of the morning on some nights and she always got me food in when she knew I was coming home from a job.

Obviously my radar is off because, in her exact words, she sees me like a brother.

A fucking brother.

No way would Denny look at me the way she does when I'd walk into a room, or when I would strip down to my gym shorts.

Needing to get this awkward exchange over with I jump out of the car and grab my box from the backseat. She's just stepping onto the curb when I reach them.

"Hey," she whispers quietly and I notice jerk's hand clench around hers. My eyes narrow on her hand. But I know Lexi. If this prick was hurting her she'd tell me. Her ex-husband beat her pretty badly so I know she wouldn't fall into the same trap. It took a lot for her to get out when she did.

I had lived next to her when I was working on a case, before the whole Davis gang issue came up. I'd been on that one for about a year before it got finished. It was the worst fucking job of my life. It's another reason I wanted out of the force.

I ended up getting drugged and one of the whores that hung around the unit used it as an invitation to sleep with me. It was the last night I had to be there too. How the fuck I got hard is anyone's guess. I'd been tested right after for every STD there is and they all came back negative.

"Hey," I nod, staring boldly at the jerk next to her.

"You remember Simon, don't you?" she asks, introducing us again.

"Hey, yeah. Nice to see you again, Steve. I was in a rush the last time," I lie. I just didn't want to have an awkward introduction. Ever since the almost kiss my ego has taken a hit. A huge fucking hit.

"It's Simon," he growls. I don't answer. Instead I look to Lexi and give her a nod before looking back to the house.

"I best be going. I've got to meet the lads in an hour," I lie. I haven't got to meet them until another four or five hours, but they don't know that.

"Okay, I'll let you go and I'll see you later. Oh, before I forget," she starts when I pass her to walk up the path. I stop walking and turn back around to face her. "A letter was posted at mine a few months back by mistake. I put it on your kitchen unit. I forgot about it until today when I sorted through my mail," she smiles.

"Cheers-"

"You have a key to his apartment?" Steve asks.

"Yeah, I look after his place," she begins to explain, but I interrupt, not wanting to get in the middle.

"I'll see you later," I nod again. "See you later, Steve."

"It's Simon," he growls again.

Well, shit. Who the fuck cares? It could be fucking Peter for all I care. All I know right now is that I want to get the fuck inside and away from them. So that's what I do. I ignore them talking at the end of the path and make my way up to the door.

The letter is the first thing I see when I walk in, but instead of heading over to pick it up I decide to crash on the couch. I switch the TV on, flicking over to Sky Sports.

TWO

KENNEDY

WHY AM I SO FUDGING nervous? He's a cop. An undercover one at that. He won't get angry. He took an oath to serve and protect, not blame and shame.

Maybe he'll be overjoyed. Yeah, he could be that.

Or not.

I groan. I'm sitting outside in my beat up red Rover. I'm still surprised it managed the half an hour trip here. It needs a bit of work done. Okay, a lot of work done to it, but it will cost me more to fix the ancient piece of poop than it would to buy a new one.

Banging my head on the steering wheel I try to calm my nerves.

I can do this. You can do this. We can do this. You have no choice but to do this.

I tell myself I'm doing the wrong thing, to turn back around, but after weeks of no replies or phone calls I demand a reason why. Imogen deserves answers.

The pent up anger I've been bottling up since it all began begins to release. Getting out of the car I wince when the rusty door protests loudly, waking up some kids in Australia. God, I should really look at doing something about that soon.

Get some WD40 or something. That should do the trick.

Locking the door, I realise I forgot to roll my window up. I'd been so nervous I began to sweat on the way over here. Groaning, I open the door again, wincing again at the sound. I start to roll the window up, but like always, it gets stuck. Not wanting to be seen next to the beat up car I quickly use my one hand to lift the glass, while the other keeps winding up the window. In no time the window is up and I'm free to lock up and move onto the curb.

Walking up to the door is easy. Knocking? That's just another flipping story. Biting my bottom lip until I taste blood, I finally find the courage to knock on the door, the sound echoing in my ears.

Anyone would think I was walking to my own death, and not what I'm about to fudging do.

When no one answers I knock again. I know he's here. I'd been waiting a few cars down for him to come home.

My nerves have only skyrocketed because I thought he was this other person. He arrived not long after I arrived. I heard him talking on the phone as he got out of his car, talking about tonight being the night and some other crude comments. When the man started walking in the direction of where I needed to go my stomach pummelled to the floor. Then I noticed a pretty woman walking from next door smiling towards him and I began to relax. But it was short lived when another car pulled up. I knew as soon as he stepped out that it was *him*.

"Yeah?" a deep, husky voice asks. I didn't even notice the door had opened. I also never expected him to look like *that*. Yeah, when he stepped out of the car my stomach did a flip, but I didn't really get a good look at him. But now... Holy fudging poop balls. What the hell did my sister do? Drug him? I know it's bad to speak ill of the dead, but in all honesty, dying had been the best thing to happen to my sister, Vicky. She had never been able to cope since my parents died. Well, even before that. She'd pop a pill or two if she failed in a lesson, and she did that a lot. After my parents she got worse. She got mixed up in things that she shouldn't have, and was spiralling out of control. There was no saving her and, believe me, I tried.

"Can I help you?" the voice asks again and I realise I'm staring. He's wearing a white shirt, his tie loose around his neck, his shirt untucked and unbuttoned a few from the top with his sleeves rolled up. He looks fudging edible.

"She's yours," I blurt out. Then close my eyes with embarrassment. *She's yours,* seriously? What the fudge is wrong with me?

"Excuse me?" he asks, looking at me like I'm a mental patient. Which I could totally be with the way I'm acting. I have the craziness for it.

"I mean, I... um... I'm Kennedy Wright," I introduce myself, forgetting my anger towards the god-like angel and the whole speech I rehearsed for the entire week.

"Hi, I'm Evan, but I still don't understand. Who are you?" A small smirk plays at his lips and my eyes are drawn to them. My belly does that flip thingy again and my body begins to heat as I stare at his lips. They're full, red and totally kissable. I reckon kissing him would be like how they kiss in the movies. You know when the bloke's lips linger, looking full against yours?

His tongue reaches out flicking his top lip, and I sigh. Yeah, kissing him would totally be like kissing a movie star.

He coughs, breaking the spell his lips had me in, and I blush furiously. I shake my head ignoring how incredibly sexy he looks when he grins and how his muscles look flexing in his white shirt.

"Get it together," I whisper.

"I'm sorry, I didn't catch that."

"Sorry. Look, can I come in?"

"Not to sound rude, Kennedy, but I still don't know why you're here or why you'd be knocking on my door. I'd remember seeing a pretty face like yours before."

He thinks I'm beautiful? Insert 'sigh' right here.

I give him a slow smile but soon lose it when I remember why I'm here.

"Do you remember Vicky Wright?" I ask.

"Vicky Wright? Vicky...Vick..., Vicky. Fuck!" he says, his eyes widening. I guess he does remember her. "Whatever the fuck that fucking bitch wants, I don't want to know about it," he snaps, going to shut the door in my face. My hand moves quickly, stopping him from slamming the door in my face. I'm shocked at my bluntness but now he's just pissed me off.

"Hold on just a darn minute," I snap, pushing at his hard chest. Even through the thin material I feel the heat scorching off him. "I'm not having you do this. You've ignored me for weeks. You had a chance to do this over the phone or by post and not face to face, so you'll hear me out."

"You're as crazy as her, are you... wait... Wright. You said you were Kennedy Wright. Please don't tell me she's your sister and she's made you come here to do her dirty work?"

"Well, as she's dead I'd say that's an astounding no," I snap.

"Fuck! I'm..."

"Please don't say you're sorry when we both know you're not," I snap, feeling my temper rising. He just holds his hands up and steps back a little, the door opening a little wider.

"If she's dead then I don't see why you're here. If she was murdered, or you want someone to look into her death, you'll have to file a report," he tells me and I turn my head to the side, studying him. He really doesn't know. I had hoped she had been lying when she told me he knew. That he didn't care.

"You don't understand. I...um... do we have to do this outside?" I ask nervously. My anger simmers. If it wasn't for Imogen then I wouldn't be here and from his reaction I'm guessing he doesn't know and it was a good thing I came.

"Come in, but if you don't hurry up and tell me what the fuck is going on, I'm going to kick you back out."

"Imogen," I blurt out nervously. I close my eyes again wishing I had some sort of control when it came to my mouth. I really know how to break news to people, I swear.

"Sorry?"

"Imogen. She's a five month old baby," I tell him straight out.

"That's...great," he tells me dryly. He's still looking at me like I've grown two heads and, for a detective or whatever, he sure doesn't know how to connect the dots.

"She's Vicky's, do the math."

He looks at me for a few seconds, just staring. Then his eyes go wide, turning a stormy grey colour and causing a shiver to run down my spine. I take a step back, my back hitting the front door.

"That fucking.... If you're insinuating what I think you are then you'll need a DNA test because that bitch spread her legs for pennies."

"You should know," I snap, hating the reminder of what she was like. Most people didn't see just how bad she was, but I did.

"I should know? I should know," he roars, pulling at his fair hair. I don't get it. What is he so mad about? Was he really that in love with her? I guess she was okay looking in a way. I don't know. All I saw when I looked at her was an underweight drug user who had no self-respect or any care for her own life and well-being. "That slut fucking drugged me. Okay, I don't know if it was her that actually slipped the drugs into my drink, but she as sure as shit was the whore that rode my dick while I was unconscious," he yells.

My eyes bug out. Oh my gosh. Is he saying what I think he's saying? No wonder he has issues and went off at me when he heard her name. He was raped. By my sister. Oh my gosh! Imogen's mom was a rapist, a drug user, a whore, and, worst of all, she was going to sell her baby for money.

"I'm sorry she did that to you," I tell him softly, my voice just above a whisper, not wanting to scare him. He seems deep in thought at the moment, his face is red with anger.

He scoffs, looking down at me. "I'm not a victim. She was as messed up as I was, if not worse. But then she was used to it whereas I had never done a drug in my life. How do you know she's mine?"

His eyes fill with tears as he sits on the edge of a thick cushioned sofa chair. Gosh, you'd get lost in that thing. I almost want to sit down in it to see if you do, but I'm not here to get comfy.

"She never told me about you. I found out. She said she had told the dad who was this big shot, but was a rat," I shrug, embarrassed I have to repeat those words. "She said you knew and even though I didn't believe her, I didn't question her. When she died they handed me her belongings. In her bag was your number with Imogen's dad, Evan, written on it."

"Fuck's sake. I need to process this. Where is the kid? How old did you say she was?"

"She's five months. She's been through a lot. She was born an addict. She was lucky that when Vicky found out she was pregnant she slowed down on the drugs, but not enough. It's how she died. She signed some papers handing her over to my care and went on her drug spree. She died two days later."

I still feel sick thinking about it. She abandoned a sick baby, her baby, to go and get her next fix. I'll never get it. She didn't even look back or hesitate. If anything, she looked relieved to be out of there.

"Is the baby okay?" he asks, but he sounds weird, robotic even.

"She is now. She got released six weeks after she was born. She's healthy. She was weaned off the drugs as soon as she was born. She had been short of breath. She was also six weeks premature but they were positive that she would make a full recovery. They did warn me about development issues but so far none have arisen.

She checks out okay."

"Good. Good," he tells me, still pacing. "When can we get the DNA test done?"

I'm actually shocked. I thought it would take me longer to convince him to see her, to take a DNA test, but he seems to be handling it alright. So far anyway. I didn't know what I'd get out of today, but Evan being so level-headed wasn't not even on my radar.

"I actually ordered one for you. I've already got Imogen's ready, but you'll need to do yours. All you have to do is take a swab sample from the inside of your cheek."

I rummage through my bag until I find the white pre-addressed envelope at the bottom and hand it to him.

"Look, I have to go. I know this has come out of the blue and you'll need some time to digest everything. I just needed to meet you to get answers. As Imogen's legal guardian, I wanted to be able to look her in the eye one day and tell her I tried," I tell him, my eyes watering. I grab the other envelope from out of the bag and hand it to him. "It's a few pictures, my phone numbers and my address for you to get in contact. Please send that off ASAP and make sure you do it right. If you do it, but don't want any part in Imogen's life, I will understand. What Vicky did, who she was, is not something to be proud of, but that little girl, she's everything light in the world. She doesn't know what her mother was like and I'll never tell her. She doesn't need to hear that the worst parts about her mother are the only parts about her."

"I'll get them done," he croaks out, his eyes watering. "I just... I need some time. I'll do anything you want me to but I just need some time to process this. If she's mine..."

"It's okay. We can talk more when we get the results back, okay?"

"Okay."

I nod my head and turn, opening the door. I hear him hit the sofa and when I turn to shut the door behind me I find him sitting down on the sofa opening the contents of the envelope I gave him. Not the one with the DNA kit in, but the other, the one with pictures of Imogen inside. I stand staring for a few more minutes, fully taking in the huge bulk of a man who begins to weep staring down at the pictures of the broken baby girl wired up in an incubator.

Something tells me I'll be hearing from Evan with the outcome being in Imogen's favour.

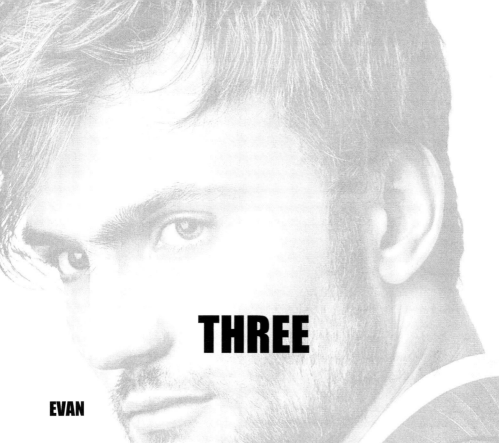

THREE

EVAN

AARON SITS BACK DOWN ON the stool in front of me, handing me another pint. I've lost count of how many drinks I've had since I arrived an hour ago. All I keep doing is replaying Kennedy's words in my mind.

I'm a dad to a five month old baby.

I stared at the pictures she gave me for hours before I realised she'd gone and the sun had gone down. I called Aaron straight away and told him I needed him to meet me.

When we met up I explained everything that had happened from the moment Kennedy arrived to the moment I snapped out of my trance. We drank. We talked. We drank some more. And now I'm ready to head over to Kennedy's and demand answers, but I don't want to scare her. I need to know why she didn't come sooner. What did her sister tell her about me? Fuck! My head is spinning just thinking about it all.

"Fuck, mate. I don't know what to say."

"A baby. A fucking baby. I don't even know if she wants me to take her. She said she came for answers, but what if that wasn't about answers at all. I don't know how to look after a baby. What if she is mine and I'm wasting more weeks until the results come in not being with her?" I ramble, scrubbing my hands down my face. I'm still in the clothes I left work in this afternoon. After Kennedy's visit everything just seems to be going downhill. My mind is torn about what to do. Do I stay away until the results are in or do I go see her? It's more time I'll miss if I wait around, but then I don't want to get attached to have it ripped away from me in a second.

For fuck's sake. I thought the woman was there hitting on me or some sort of stripper the guys had hired. I wouldn't put it past my ex work colleagues to do something like that. She looked so fucking cute all flustered and shy, staring at me like she was trying to find the first place to lick. It was the only giveaway she had given that made me think she wasn't a stripper. Looks wise, she's a fucking knockout.

Then she got all feisty, pushing me with her dainty finger. She's like a little pixie fairy, all small and shit. Her fucking eyes were the colour of melted chocolate. They were deep, rich and so fucking sexy it made me want to drag her back to my room and do unspeakable things to her.

"Man, you'll figure this shit out. It probably ain't your kid anyway," he tells me. I swear he's had that exact speech on repeat since I told him the news. Aaron is my best mate; I'd jump in front of a bullet for him. In fact, he'd do the same for me. But when it comes to advice, he really does fucking suck.

I'd have gone to my sister but she still isn't talking to me after the whole keeping my job a secret. I'd done it for a few reasons, but mostly it because we weren't allowed to tell people what we do.

It also didn't help that I could have prevented Carl from kidnapping her. I didn't know he was going to do it, but I knew he was up to something. We were just waiting for it to go down. If I knew she was involved I would have put a stop to him before.

I've sent her bloke, Mason, a message tonight asking him to talk to her on my behalf. I need her now more than ever. It's selfish of me because since I joined up with the agency I've done nothing but avoid anything family related. When I have seen them I've kept everything bottled up.

Anyway, he finally replied half an hour ago saying he'd talk to her for me, but I needed to give her time.

Never thought I'd let my little sister date a fucker like him. The lad has slept with more people than the entire police force in my department put together. He's a fucking animal. Or he was. I've been keeping an eye on him when he's not with Denny and, so far, the lad doesn't even blink in another girl's direction.

It's a fucking miracle after the rumours I've heard about him.

My sister, though, she's a game changer. She's kind, sweet, loving, and doesn't want to change you. All she wants is honesty, love, and commitment. So I can see why Mason only sees her. She's once in a life time kind of girl.

"I don't fucking know," I groan, my thoughts directing back to Kennedy and the little girl. My little girl. There was something in the way Kennedy looked at me, the way she spoke about Imogen, that has me believing the kid is mine. A strong feeling overwhelmed me when she announced I had a daughter. It rocked through my body and I just knew. I don't fucking know. For all I know the woman could be just like her slut of a sister. She most likely is. But remembering the way she looked, dressed and spoke, I know immediately it's the pissed off side of me talking. She's nothing like her sister.

Oh well! The tests will be done and I'll finally know the answers that can put my mind at rest. A part of me hopes that she is mine. I don't want to imagine who her father is otherwise. I knew most of the blokes at that unit through my job, getting to know them, and let's just say, they are the worst of the worst. That little girl deserves more than a father and a mother coming from a world like that.

"Well, drink up. Everyone just walked in," Aaron announces and I straighten on my stool.

"It's supposed to be a fucking surprise. We said eight, dipshit," William, my old boss, says, glaring at Aaron. I chuckle but it's forced. I'm not going to be much fun tonight, but I know the guys wanted to give me a proper send off, so for them I can fake it and drink until my mind is blank.

"He called me up," Aaron defends with his hands in the air.

"Useless fucking shit," William mutters, then steps out the way when Dave walks over with a tray of Jagerbombs.

"Shots!" he yells and I wince. The noise was loud enough in here already but now that these bunch of shits have joined the party, it's turned to deafening.

Fuck, if that isn't a clear sign that I'm getting old, I don't know what is.

Just as I thought the night was getting better the fucking reception slut walks in with one of the new lads. Mikey I think I heard his name was. He's hanging onto her every word. Poor fucker is going to regret it once he gets to know her better, or worse, sleeps with her.

Aaron notices where I'm looking and groans.

"I swear, I didn't invite the bitch, but if it helps, I'll put twenty on it not lasting another hour. The poor fuck looks miserable."

I look again and notice he does look fucking miserable. He's eyeing up one of the women that have been standing up by the bar all night.

"Half an hour and make it thirty," I laugh, shaking his hand. He laughs with me, and we pick up our shots, ignoring Dave as he counts down from three.

Does he think we're at school?

When another tray of shots appears I know I'm in for a long night. Kidneys, may you rest in peace, my friends.

The night ventures on and it's one in the morning when the guys finally carry me out of the pub.

"I'm never drinking again," I whine, my words slurring.

"That's what you said the last time we went out," one of the guys laughs, but I don't find it funny. The room is spinning, or I'm spinning. I don't know. I'm too wasted to tell the difference.

"Let's get you home," William rumbles, his voice sounding more slurred than mine. I'm shoved into a taxi and Aaron hops in beside me giving the driver my address.

I must have fallen asleep because I'm shaken awake when we pull up outside mine. "You kipping the night?" I ask Aaron.

"Yeah, mate. Wouldn't want you to choke on your own vomit now, would we?"

"If he' sick in my cab, you pay," the driver shouts, his voice foreign.

"I'm kidding."

"He's not. I feel green," I joke, but end up choking.

"You, you get out my cab," I hear yelled as Aaron pulls me out. The door slams behind us and the taxi speeds away, the tyres screeching on the tarmac.

"Ha, joke's on that fucker. We haven't paid," Aaron hoots.

"Ha, take that, ya fucker," I shout down the empty road. The taxi isn't even in sight but I don't care.

"Come on, Rocky," Aaron teases.

He drags me up the path at the same time Lexi opens her door. "Is everything okay?" she asks timidly, her eyes scanning Aaron up and down. They've met a few times so I'm used to this interaction, but fuck me if I don't roll my eyes.

"Peachy, go back to Steve," I tell her, snarky, wondering why her life got so perfect while mine got so fucked up.

"Um, it's Simon and we broke up," she tells me softly. I feel like shit. Even if Steve was a jerk, she doesn't deserve this. We walk through the front door, me wobbling on my feet.

"Sorry. The guy was a dick."

"Yeah, he was," she smiles, looking at me with concern.

"Well, I'm going to bed. You two play nice," I scowl and then walk head first into the doorframe, banging my head across it.

"Fuck!" I roar. Shit, that fucking hurt. "Who put that there?"

"Careful, mate," Aaron laughs and I turn to him, giving him a hateful glare. I move through the bungalow, down the corridor and into my bedroom.

The results need to hurry the fuck up and arrive already. I need to know. And I need to know now. Otherwise I'll end up being this drunk every night until they arrive.

I hear voices coming from down the hall and I groan into my pillow. Looks like Lexi isn't leaving any time soon. The door to my room opens, letting light in, and a deep chuckle echoes around the room.

"Fuck off," I grumble, my face shoved into the pillow. The fucker turns the light on, and I know it's on fucking purpose.

Whatever he must see must satisfy him because the next thing I hear is him clicking the light off and shutting the door behind him. I hear him address Lexi, asking if she wants to stay for some coffee.

My head is spinning but I manage to drown out their yapping and end up drifting into a deep sleep, my thoughts consumed by a baby I haven't even met.

FOUR

KENNEDY

"COME ON, BABY GIRL, GO TO sleep," I coo softly in Imogen's ear. She's started teething. No matter how many freaking text books I've read or looked up online for ways to help her, nothing is fudging working. My heart is literally breaking hearing her in so much pain. It's only taken me five months to decipher her cries. Each cry sounds different and are for different things.

She cries loudly in my arms. The chunky, healthy bundle is pulling at her now red ears. I sit down in the rocking chair and take her temperature.

Just a little over the normal temperature, but it still doesn't ease my worry.

Knowing I'm not going to be able to get much sleep this morning I start rocking backwards and forwards. My mouth opens and the lyrics to *Meghan Trainor's All About That Bass*, rolls out. It's the first song to pop into my head. Most likely because it's always playing on the radio.

After the first verse she starts to settle. Her tiny but chubby fist is shoved into her mouth, the other still holding onto her ear.

Thankfully, it's not long before she's asleep and I place her gently down in her cot. I'm glad I don't have to work this week. I had some annual leave left. It felt right using it with Imogen being so poorly. I can't afford to have any unpaid time off.

Tip toeing out of her tiny room so I don't wake her, I walk back through my small, two bedroomed flat to the kitchen. The place isn't ideal but it's the only place I could find that was affordable.

It's located in one of the roughest places in town and I do hate it here. I'm never able to get a full night's sleep due to loud music coming from other floors, or because some couple decided tonight's the night to get into a fight. Imagine that echoing around your flat at God knows what time of night.

Loud banging at the door has me jumping out of my skin. I quickly drop the washing-up liquid and run to the door before they can wake up Imogen.

If it's my creepy neighbour from along the hall I'm going to cry. I'm pretty sure he does drugs and, I swear, when he *conveniently* knocks on my door it's always for sugar. I'm pretty sure it's really to see if I have any valuables lying around that he can rob when I'm not here. Luckily, I'm not one for splurging out on things. I have second-hand goods from charity shops and keep my mother's jewellery locked away in a box under my bed.

"I don't have any spare-" I'm cut off when a large hand wraps around my throat, pushing me back into the flat. He's squeezing so tight I don't have a chance to breathe in and scream. The door slams and my first thought is hoping Imogen doesn't wake up. I don't want whoever this is to know she's here. I'm shaking uncontrollably as I claw at the man's wrists.

My eyes open wide when the scruff of a man slams me back against the door, his eyes red and furious.

"Where's my fucking money, bitch?"

I try to talk, I really do, but his hand is cutting off any air I had left in my lungs. I frantically claw at his wrists to get him to loosen his hold, but it never happens. Wheezing noises start to leave my mouth causing me to panic.

What the hell is happening? Who is he? What money? Does he think I'm someone else? I look around, for what I don't know. It's not like I can get away from him to get anything. His hold is too strong.

My vision begins to blur just as he drops me to the floor. I stumble back a few steps, my mind frozen. I don't even have a chance to think, to speak, or to catch my breath before his hand clashes with my cheek. Pain radiates down my face, tears finally falling free, and I cry out in pain.

"Please," I beg, for what I'm not sure. I just hope he understands I'm not who he thinks I am.

"Get the fuck up, bitch," he sneers.

When I don't move fast enough he grips me by the hair, lifting me and pinning me back to the door. The force of my hip hitting the door handle has me screaming out in pain.

His fingers dig into my cheeks making the throbbing from his backhand throb harder. It feels like I have an orange stuck on the inside of my skin, it feels that tight and swollen. The pain is something I've never felt before.

Never in my life have I been so scared. My whole body is shaking with it. How could someone do this to someone else?

"Please, I don't know who you are," I cry out pleading with him, but it ends up sounding like a squeak instead.

"Your sister owes me three grand. I want my fucking money, bitch."

What? Oh my Lord. The letters. A few months after my sister died I started receiving letters demanding money. I just thought it was for one of the neighbours and, because it wasn't addressed to anyone, I just threw them out. I didn't even think much of it. I was too worried about Imogen being in the hospital.

"She's... She's dead," I wheeze out, my voice hitching.

"I know that, you fucking whore. You're my payment. You were what your sister put down as, shall we call it, a *guarantor*," he snickers.

"I don't understand," I wheeze through. I don't have that kind of money. I live by my monthly cheques and that's it. I don't have any kind of savings anywhere.

"Let me put this straight. You're basically fucking screwed if you don't pay up."

I look into his dead eyes and can feel he's deadly serious. What did I ever do to deserve this and why would my *sister* do this to me? Before I have a chance to explain the situation he throws me to the floor with force and I land on the coffee table, the cheap wood breaking under my weight.

Coughing, I roll onto my side only for his boot to land in my side.

"Please stop. Someone, help!" I scream out, my body shaking with more than fear. A sickening feeling overcomes my body and by the time he's finished landing another two blows to my stomach, he bends down on one knee, his face only inches away from mine.

I'm completely out of breath and unbearable pain spreads through my entire body. A horrible, tight, cramping sensation pulses in my stomach and I have to swallow back bile.

"If I don't get that money in a month that little brat in there is going to get fucking sold to the highest bidder," he sneers and before I can fight back, or get to Imogen, or even plead with him, his fist lands in my face, my whole world turning black.

Sometime later I awaken by gentle hands shaking my shoulders. My whole body is throbbing; an agonising pain pounding hits through my body.

I slowly open my eyes, and when I see my neighbour who lives across the hall, everything that happened slowly slams into me at once.

"Imogen," I cry out, hearing her crying.

"Don't move. I'll get her, Kennedy."

I couldn't be more thankful for Melanie than I am in this moment. Not only has she been the only neighbour I get on with, but she's also a lifesaver and a friend.

She walks in with Imogen still crying in her arms. When I put my hands up for her I cry out in pain.

"I've got her. What happened? Shall I call the police?" she asks concerned, her words rushed.

I shake my head not knowing what to do or say. Will it make it worse going to the police? Of course it will. And what can the police do? It's not like I have proof. Hell, I don't even know who that man is. He could be anyone. All I know is that my sister was connected to him.

"What are you doing here?" I ask, trying hard to keep the tears at bay. Melanie said she was leaving for a few weeks for a job. She isn't meant to be back for another week.

"I'll tell you later. I came over because this must have come during the week," she says, handing me a white envelope. I take it out of her hand. I'm just about to throw it to the side and take a still crying Imogen from Mel, when the top of the envelope catches my attention.

"Oh my," I gasp, tearing the letter open. My eyes flicker over numbers, words, and it isn't until I get to the centre page that the words I have been hoping for are written in bold letters.

"What is it?" Melanie asks concerned, still rocking a crying Imogen in her arms.

"He's her dad," I gasp, then burst into tears. He can protect her. But then I will lose her. The thought has bile rising in my throat. What if he doesn't want her? What am I going to do?

I hold my hands up, my tears running freely down my face. I need her. I just need to hold her, to make sure she's okay. I don't know if he touched her. My sore body screams in agony when Mel finally relents and hands me Imogen. I finally have her in my arms. As soon as I breathe in her baby scent I burst into a fit of more tears.

My tears only make Imogen cry harder and, even with my sore body, I try my hardest to soothe her.

"It's okay, baby. Everything is going to be okay. I'll protect you, I promise," I promise her. And I will. Even if it means I have to give her up to her father in order to do that. It will kill me, but I will.

"What is going on, Kennedy?" Melanie asks, sitting down next to me. "Who did this to you? I ran to get some ice from mine before you came through, but it seems neither of us have anything frozen." Her tone sounds light, but I can hear the underlying worry hidden beneath.

"Someone... Someone attacked me. He wants money. Money I don't have. He's going to take Imogen if I don't," I cry. The same paralysing fear, thinking about that man hits me once again and I begin to shake.

"Has this got anything to do with your sister?" Melanie asks. She knows all about my sister and my family. I don't know what I would have done without her help when I first got Imogen home. Mel has two kids of her own that are fully grown and now moved out and have their own families. Her advice has been a godsend.

"I'm scared," I admit, crying. "Shush, Imogen. I promise everything is going to be okay," I tell her, hoping to God I'm right.

"WHAT THE FUCK HAS HAPPENED HERE?" is roared. My whole body locks up tight, thinking *he* has come back to finish what he started. When my fear filled eyes look up, I'm hit with something much, much worse.

"Evan," I breathe.

FIVE

EVAN

I T'S BEEN WEEKS SINCE I sent off the DNA test and even though I knew it would take some time, I never thought it would be this long.

"You need to snap out of it, mate. You've been off with the fairies for weeks," Harris, another one of my best mates, tells me.

He doesn't even realise how close he is about the fairy comment. I've not been able to stop myself from thinking about Kennedy or Imogen, since I was told.

"I'm just going to go home, I'm sorry."

"It's okay. You can take the week off anyway. I'll get everything sorted. Just make sure you get your head cleared before you come back." I go to interrupt but he stops me, holding his hand up. "This is how accidents happen, Evan. Your head isn't in the game."

"I know. Just give me a few days," I groan and then leave him to fill out the paperwork on the Court's file.

I'm pulling up outside mine and a sense of deja vu hits me when I see Lexi walking down the path, hand in hand with some new tool. What surprises me is that it isn't Aaron. After the night I got completely wasted I thought the two had kicked it off. Obviously not.

I jump out of the car giving her a chin lift, not wanting to go through the same pleasantries as last time.

"Hey," she smiles, and I notice the tool looking at me like I'm competition. *Don't worry, loser, I have enough problems.*

"Hey," I nod.

"This is Steve," she introduces, and I want to groan and look to the sky. Why does she constantly put me through this shit?

"I need to run in and get a file, but it's good to see you, and you, Simon," I nod and walk off.

"It's Steve," he shouts back and I shake my head confused. I nod my head towards him before turning back around and head inside. The door jams and I notice the mail wedging under the door. Pulling it out, I walk through flicking through it.

"Bills, junk, bills, bills, junk, wrong address, junk, junk, oh fuck," I gasp when I get to the last one. I rip it open but as I'm about to pull it out I close up and freeze. I'm not prepared to read what it says on that letter. I'm confused on what I want it to say. On the one hand I want her to be mine, but the other part doesn't want her to be. I wanted to have children when I had finally settled down with a woman I loved, and not by some woman who took advantage.

Closing my eyes, I pull the letter out and open it up. I count to ten before reopening them and look down. Nothing makes sense to me until I see it written in bold black writing. I am Imogen Wright's biological father.

"Fuck!"

Needing to meet her, I quickly run to my room, not wanting to waste another minute of not knowing my daughter. I grab the envelope with the pictures of Imogen and the address and run to the door, grabbing my keys on the way.

So far I've managed to only turn back twice. The first was because I didn't call ahead and the second is because I didn't bring her a gift.

The minute I let my mind focus on what was happening I finally realised how much I want this. Imogen may not be with the woman I love, but she's still my flesh and blood.

I'm a fucking dad.

A fucking dad.

I'm not going to end up like my father, neglecting my kid, so I got her the fluffiest pink pony teddy bear I could find. I guess the second time those thoughts raced through my mind I knew I needed to stop off somewhere and grab something.

After getting Imogen's pony I get back in the car and head in the direction of Kennedy's. When I pull up into her estate I'm more than certain Imogen being mine is a blessing. The woman lives in a fucking shithole of a place. It's the worst place to live around here. I must have been out of it, because her address didn't register until I got here.

I get out of my Audi and grab the pony from out of the boot before locking the car up and flicking the alarm on. I look around, hoping there isn't anyone watching. I don't trust anyone not to attempt to take it. The car is mint. She's also my baby.

Not anymore, my inner brain screams, reminding me of Imogen.

I'm just about to press the buzzer for her door when someone walks out, leaving the door open for me. I head over to the lift trying not to gag from the smell of stale piss stinking the place out.

I hurry up and get in the lift, not that it's much better, but fuck if it gets me closer to where I want to be. Maybe I can talk Kennedy to come and take a walk. Get some fresh air. Nothing about inhaling the toxic air around us can be classed as healthy. I'm worried I'm going to catch something just visiting.

Looking at the door numbers I notice Kennedy's door is wide open and I head over. What I expected was nothing compared to what I found. On the floor, holding a screaming baby was, Kennedy. The place was a mess. A table lay broken in the middle of the floor, but what had me raging were the bruises covering her pale, tear stricken face.

"WHAT THE FUCK HAS HAPPENED HERE?" I roar, stepping into the room. I watch as Kennedy's body visibly tenses, her hands shaking with fear. The older lady next to her moves to shield them, looking at me with fright.

"I think you need to leave. I've called the police," the lady I don't know shouts. I look at her curiously and wonder who the hell she thinks I am.

"Mel, this is…"

"Someone who wants to know what the fuck has happened," I interrupt, stepping farther into the room. From the door her face looked bad, but on a closer look it's worse, and I can tell by the way she winces while rocking the baby back and forth that it's more than her face that is hurting her.

"Who are you?" Mel, the lady, asks. What a loaded question. Who am I?

"This is Imogen's biological father," Kennedy whispers, her voice sounding tired. I walk over, ignoring the death glare Mel is giving me, and kneel down beside Kennedy. My eyes look over her face and I can't help but clench my fists. Who the fuck did this?

"What happened?" I ask in a softer voice.

Instead of answering me she breaks down into tears, handing me Imogen. At first I don't know what to do and I hold her at arm's length.

Fuck, she's got some lungs on her.

I hold her closer, her head resting on my shoulder, and do what I've watched Denny do with Hope and start bouncing her and patting her gently on the bum.

It's not long before she stops crying and only cute little noises escape. It's then that I start to enjoy the moment.

I'm a dad!

I hold her a little tighter and it's in this moment I know I'll never be able to leave her again. Not even for a night. But hell if I know what I'm doing, especially when her mom, so to speak, is hot as fucking hell and is obviously in some kind of abusive relationship.

"You have to take her, to protect her," comes a strangled sob, and I look to Kennedy confused. Mel starts rubbing her back affectionately but soon stops when she realises it's only hurting Kennedy more.

"You need to tell me what's happened here. Did your boyfriend hurt you?"

She looks up to me wide eyed. "No. I don't have a boyfriend," she cries, becoming hysterical. "Someone came here. He hurt me. He said my sister owed him three grand. I don't have that kind of money. He said that I'm the insurance she gave him to get his money back if she couldn't. If I don't pay him back he'll take Imogen and sell her. You have to take her and get her as far away from me as possible," she sobs. Her expression completely breaks and I know just asking me to take Imogen is breaking her heart. Her words tug and my heart, seeing her so broken triggers something inside me and for the first time in my life I want to take care of someone other than myself.

"Tell me exactly what he said," I demand, going into work mode.

"That's pretty much it. Oh, and I've got a month." She tries to wipe her tears away but more just keep coming. She looks to me, her eyes wide. "Oh my, you got her to sleep," she says softly before bursting into more tears.

"Hey, don't cry."

"I don't want to lose her, but I have to. I can't protect her."

"And what about you? Who's going to protect you?" I ask her.

"No one."

She looks tired and worn out, so I do the only thing I can do. "Get up and go and get yours and Imogen's stuff packed."

"Huh?" she breathes, looking at me all confused.

"Just do it. I need to make a phone call," I tell her, harsher than intended.

"Come on, I'll help you," Melanie offers, helping Kennedy to her feet. I look at her face and can tell she's in a world of pain. It just makes me want to hunt down this fucker all the more. No one threatens innocent women or children and gets away with it.

What the hell is going on with me?

Once they're out of sight I look down at Imogen properly for the first time and smile. She has my button nose, the poor thing. I don't know whose colour eyes she has 'cause she's sleeping, but I remember Vicky had light blue eyes, whereas I have dark brown.

She's so tiny, so innocent, curled up on my chest, that the thought of someone ever hurting her actually makes me want to do a life sentence in prison for murder.

I dial William's number knowing I'm going to need help on this one, and my old files. He answers on the third ring.

"'Ello. Miss us already?"

"Jackass, and no. Look, I need a favour."

A loud booming laugh erupts through the phone and I have to pull my ear away for a second. "You've been gone a few weeks and already you want a favour."

"Okay, can you just fast track my old files over please? I need everything we have on the drug bust we did on the Carmack's." I can't be doing with his banter or teasing digs at the moment. I need answers. I need to know who is doing this and why. The only thing I can come up with is Vicky's past. That unit was her past.

"What? Why? We closed that case."

Like I need reminding that we closed that case. It was the worst job I had ever been undercover for and never been so relieved when we finally closed it.

"Look, there's a lot I need to explain, but right now all you need to know is that someone from that case has threatened someone... close to me," I hesitate, the word love nearly popping out of mouth. Thinking about it, it only took one glance at the little rugrat and I was in love. Imogen stirs in my arms and I rock her gently so that she doesn't wake.

"Okay, is there something you need me to do?" he asks without hesitation. That's the only thing so far that I've missed about my old job. How they have your back. Not that Harris doesn't, it's just that he asks questions first, not later. I suppose we have a lot to figure out before we get to where we need to be.

"Not yet, but I'll keep you posted. Give me an hour and I'll be home," I tell him before ending the call. I walk towards the hushed voices and into Kennedy's room. It's not anything like I had pictured. It's plain, boring, and not even decorated. I expected colour, lots of colour. But then, I don't really know her and she's obviously struggling if she's living in this shithole.

"Can you take Immy so I can go get her cot and stuff down? I'll call a friend to come and get it all. Unless you want me to buy her new ones?" I ask, not thinking about what Immy might not have. For all I know she could just have the basics, but what do I know. I don't even know what a baby needs and from what I know so far about Kennedy, she doesn't seem like the person to neglect a kid.

"What? What's going on? Are you taking her?" she asks, her face scrunched up and ready to blow. Even after asking me, the thought of Immy being taken away from her is killing her from the inside. I can officially say I know how she feels because just thinking of never seeing the cute little bundle, that has captured my heart with a second of meeting her, is killing me.

"No," I start and watch her body relax. "I'm taking both of you. You're coming to live with me," I tell her. I don't even know where that came from, but now the words are out of my mouth I realise I mean them. When I first told her to pack her stuff I was going to send them to a friend's, or somewhere safe.

"What? No. You can't do that. We can't do that?"

"Do you want protection? Do you want Immy safe? Do you want to be safe?"

"Of course..."

"Then, there you go. Now take Immy, please."

"Immy?" she asks, her face crinkled, looking cute. "Her name is Imogen."

"Sorry, I guess it just slipped out," I wince, wondering if she thinks I'm taking over. I don't want to take Imogen off her but I do want to be with her at all times. Imogen, that is. Not that I would mind Kennedy's company if she offered it. It's then that I inwardly groan. I have to live with her now. I have to see her naked, half naked, and dressed on a daily basis. She's going to be in my space all the time.

I've never had that before.

Calm down, she could have loads of bad habits. It's true. She could. My sister had a million and one.

"No, it's fine. I like it," she smiles, but it doesn't reach her eyes.

An hour later we're pulling up to mine. After speaking to Harris about what was going on he made a point for me to leave as much clothing and shit as I could at the apartment. So I did, and instead of bringing her cot with us as planned, I called up Baby Care and ordered everything a baby her age would need. I even paid fast track delivery for today and they will also be assembling all of the furniture. That's another thing out the way so I can concentrate on finding out who did this to Kennedy. She's still pretty shaken up and when we walk inside I walk her down the hall to my bedroom.

"Here. You need to lie down. I'll go get you some Ibuprofen."

"No, I should be awake for when Imogen wakes up," she argues, but I notice her hands still shaking.

"Go run yourself a bath. I have one right down the hall. Please, just go have a bath. When you come back out I'll have a look at those bruises your shirt's been hiding."

"How..."

"I can tell by the way you're walking. Let me just check you don't need to go to the hospital, then you can take some painkillers and go to sleep for a bit. You'll feel much better for it."

"Imogen needs a bottle in half an hour, though."

"Just go," I tell her, giving her a gentle push in the direction of the bathroom. I quickly tell her where the spare towels are then head back down to the kitchen and begin unpacking the bags I know have all of Imogen's bottles and stuff in. I put the car seat, with Imogen still in it, down by the door and get to work before one of the boys brings the files over.

Placing everything I can on the kitchen worktop, I'm stunned to silence at everything in front of me. There's this round machine thingy that has these nipple things in them. A bunch of different size bottles, lids, and more nipple thingies.

A plastic tub of baby formula sits to the edge and I smile.

I can do this.

How hard can making a bottle really be?

Ten minutes later Kennedy emerges from the bathroom looking hot. Literally hot. She looks like she's been sitting in a sauna for the past hour instead of taking a bath for the past ten.

"You okay?" I ask, but end up choking on my words when she walks around the counter wearing a baggy t-shirt that barely covers her ass. She's wearing boxers underneath but it does nothing to keep my mind from wandering.

Fuck, for a small person she has pretty amazing legs and I can't help but imagine what they'd feel like wrapped around me.

"Are you okay?" she asks quizzically, then starts to chuckle. "You have baby milk down your shirt."

I look down to find she's right. Damn. "Yeah, I'm just trying to figure this shit out," I tell her, nodding to the powered milk.

"Here, I'll show you," she tells me, her face scrunching up in pain when she moves towards me. Knowing I need to learn, I ignore her pain for a second and watch as she puts together the bottle, starts to boil some water, and then assembles the machine with the nipples in it.

"This is the steriliser. The bottles need to be sterilised after each use to keep them clean. I only make more than one bottle up during the night. I just leave the boiled water in the bottle until she wakes up. Then I add the milk like so," she starts, and shows me how to put the right amount of powder into the bottle. I'm so amazed by everything that I can't take my eyes off her.

When I notice she's not moving any more I turn to look at her, finding her staring back at me with a pink blush to her cheeks.

"What?" I ask confused.

"I said: Where do you keep the jug?"

"Oh, here," I tell her, pointing over her head. I reach up to the cabinet and grab the plastic jug down for her. She fills it with cold water then plops the bottle inside it.

"All done," she smiles. "Just let that cool down to lukewarm so it doesn't burn Imogen's mouth and you're good to go."

"I can do that."

She gives me a blinding smile and we both stand there staring at each other awkwardly. When Imogen breaks the silence by waking up we shake our heads. We both move at the same time, both of us pausing before going for her again.

"Go on, you go. I'll just go...um...lie down. Do you have those painkillers?"

she asks timidly, looking shy as hell.

"Yeah, here," I tell her and walk over to the tablets I'd gotten ready in the mix of making myself look like the milk powder monster.

She takes them from me and swallows them dry. I watch as her throat bobs up and down and I end up swallowing a gulp myself. My brain thinks of what her throat would look like swallowing something else but I clear it straight away.

Fuck, this is going to kill me. I quickly grab Imogen out of the car seat and smile down at her. She's so freaking cute. She even has my eyes.

My heart warms and for once in my life I feel like I'm right where I needed to be. I know for a fact I'm never going to let her down, ever.

In the short amount of time I've known I was a dad, I've managed to move her in and make a bottle by myself. Okay, not by myself, but the thought was there.

"She'll need changing and the bottle's ready. Just make sure when you check the temp, do it on the inside of your wrist," Kennedy tells me before slowly walking out of the room. I look to Imogen with wide eyes.

A part of me is hoping she meant change as in a change of clothes. But then I shift my face closer and take a big sniff and I know she's on about her nappy.

I groan and grab the bag I noticed Kennedy filling with nappies and a changing mat and walk into the front room, making sure to grab the bottle.

"Come on, little one. Help a man out, okay?" I ask Imogen who is now stripped down to just her nappy. Whoever the fuck made those vests were *not* thinking of kids when they designed them. I thought at one point I was going to break her arm getting it out of the thing.

To the left I have baby wipes, nappy bags, and a peg. Check. To the right I have the nappy and clean baby grow. It's amazing what you pick up being around your sister. Thank fuck she had a child at eighteen or I'd be fucked right now.

It's not like it's going to be hard, but, just in case something does go wrong, I have a spare nappy on standby.

I take in one deep breath before beginning what will now be my life.

SIX

KENNEDY

THE BED EVEN SMELLED LIKE him. I couldn't escape his intoxicating scent and it was nearly driving me crazy. I toss and turn for a second, not able to get comfy, when I start to hear Imogen fussing.

I still can't believe he's already so hands on. He hasn't even questioned himself and has taken it all in his stride. I really admire him for that. Most men would use the excuse they don't know what they're doing to get out of anything and everything, but not Evan. He seems to actually know what he's doing or at least tries to.

I'm still in shock he's offered for us to move in. I know I'm only extended in that invitation because of Imogen, but either way I'm thankful. I know for a fact I wouldn't feel safe sleeping in that flat after everything that's happened.

Just remembering the pressure from his kicks and the force of his punches has tears slipping free. I can't believe someone could be cruel enough to do what he did to me today. It just doesn't seem real. None of it does. The threats, the beating, and the moving in, it all feels too much. Even Evan being so understanding about everything is all too much. He has every right to hate me right now. I've put his daughter at risk. My sister put her at risk. But he seems to be dealing with everything okay.

I hear Imogen fussing again and knowing I won't be able to sleep with everything going on, no matter how exhausted I feel, I get up and slowly creep out the bedroom door. I walk the short distance down the hall and look into the living room. There on the floor of the living room, is Evan, with an irritated Imogen wiggling.

I cover my mouth to muffle my giggle when I take him in. He's got a peg pinned to his nose, washing-up gloves on, and is currently dry heaving as he wipes the remains of poop from Imogen's bum.

"Nooooo," he whisper yells and I take step forward; worried. Ignoring the pain in my side I bend forward a little to look closer and burst out laughing. His head snaps to me and his shoulders slump with defeat. "She just pissed on me."

"She's marking her territory," I giggle. "Trust me, it's when she poops in the bath you have to worry," I tell him, hoping to make him feel better.

"She doesn't?" he gasps, horrified.

"Oh, she does," I giggle.

"How do I get this on?" he grumbles.

Instead of doing it I sit down next to him and point to the sticky labels at the end of the nappy. "That end always goes under the bum."

He follows my instructions and in no time has her nappy on and, for some reason, her bed clothes. "You do know you'll need to dress her again after she has a bath."

"You said to get her changed. I didn't know if you meant nappy or clothes an d,   because she pooped I thought I'd do both." He shrugs like it's no big deal. I go to tell him how thankful I am when a loud banging noise startles me and I immediately move closer to Evan. Does the bloke know I moved and that I've got help? Is he going to take Imogen? A squeaking noise escapes the back of my throat.

Scared out of my mind, I don't notice Evan moving until he's kneeling in front of me, holding a wiggly Imogen.

"Hey, it's okay. It's a friend from work. He's brought me everything to do with the case involving your sister. Okay?"

My tensed shoulders relax and I give him a nod. I know all about the case he worked on. Vicky called him a rat and did nothing but scream about him after she got arrested. I'm surprised he didn't have her down for a rape charge. That's what it was in my eyes. Rape. I'm about to ask what that case has to do with it when he moves, getting up to answer the door.

Feeling self-conscious, I get up and sit down on the chair. It's as comfy as I imagined the first time I saw it. Feeling bold I kick my feet up, tucking them underneath me, and lean my head back against the back pillow.

Hearing voices at the door I close my eyes and try to relax, but tiredness overrides me and I fall into a deep sleep.

Sometime later I wake up in a bed and not on the sofa where I was the last time I remember being awake.

What the sugar?

Getting up I notice I'm back in Evan's room and begin to blush. We don't even know each other and he's let me take over his space. I groan when I find I'm half naked wearing a large t-shirt I've never seen before. Sniffing the t-shirt I feel lightheaded. It smells of masculinity, sex and of Evan.

Only just realising that he must have undressed me, I get up from the bed noticing it's turned dark outside. I can't see a clock in the room, but it feels late. Stepping out of bed I grab a loose pair of pyjama bottoms and head out to find Evan. When he's not in the kitchen or living area I begin to panic.

Rushing back towards the bedroom I notice a soft glow coming from another room. Walking closer I hear a hum of a voice.

"We may not have known each other long, but I promise you there will nothing you don't know about me. You've got me now," I hear Evan whisper in a soft voice I've not heard him use yet.

I step quietly towards the door and peeping through the gap, I gasp. The room is beautiful. A cot lays in one corner with a pink princess canopy. He has a new rocking chair which he's sitting in currently, holding a bottle to Imogen's mouth. Looking closer I'd say he's been in here awhile. He has a mug of something hot on the table next to him along with a pile of folders and papers.

What on earth is all that? And why is he reading them at this time?

"Hey, you're awake."

I jump hearing his husky, deep voice. "I'm sorry. I didn't mean to fall asleep. I can't believe I slept through all of this," I whisper ashamedly.

"Are you hungry? I ordered a takeout. It's in the microwave. I'm sorry I didn't wake you, but you seemed like you needed the sleep. Plus, when I did try to wake you up you didn't move an inch," he tells me and I feel blush rise on my cheeks.

Sugar puffs!

How embarrassing. "I guess I didn't stir when you got me changed either."

"About that," he says sheepishly. "I'm sorry. It's just my sister hates sleeping in her clothes. We went away once on holiday and she forgot her pyjamas. We spent the whole night trying to find somewhere that was open because she refused to sleep in her t-shirts."

"Oh, it's okay," I smile and look down at Imogen who's soundly sucking on her bottle and looking up at Evan with big doe eyes. "How has she been?"

"She's been really good. She was a little groggy earlier but I picked her up and she calmed down," he whispers looking down at her. He looks freaking cute holding her. Imogen is a tiny baby, but looking at her in Evan's arms makes her look even smaller. And, if I'm being honest, he looks hot as hell holding her.

"I'm going to take her back to the doctors," I sigh, wondering if it's more than teething. She's been getting a temperature on and off. It's times like this I wish my mom were here to get advice from, but she's not.

"What? Why? Did I do something wrong?" he asks panicked, his eyes scanning Imogen from head to toe.

"No! No. She's been like this for a week now. She's been so off. She's usually a happy, peaceful baby, but lately she's been so upset, like she's in pain. I took her last Tuesday and they said it's teething but I don't know," I shrug, stroking my finger down her cheek. Her eyes focus on me and she starts flapping her arms excitedly. I laugh along with Evan.

"I think someone's excited to see you," he laughs.

I take her from him and smile widely at her. She's everything to me. She's my world and on the days that everything gets to me, she is my reason to keep going. I love her like my own. In fact, the older she gets, the more I've wanted to call myself her mum. A few times it's slipped out and every time I've felt guilty in a way. She deserves to have that in her life, though, to call someone mum. But now with Evan in the picture, and him being the biological father, I need to find out what he'll think about it first.

"Let me know when you want to go the doctors. I'll come with you," he smiles, picking up a large file.

"What's all that?" I ask and realise how rude I'm being. We don't even know each other. "I'm sorry, that was rude. You don't have to tell me anything."

I look down to find Imogen sleeping soundly on my shoulder, a loud burp escaping her mouth. I chuckle quietly as Evan answers.

"Don't worry about it, it's fine. If you want to pop Immy in the cot, we can talk in the front room." He gets up, picking up the stack of files with him, and walks the two steps over to me, kissing Immy on the head. His scent overwhelms my senses and my knees begin to shake. "I'm so glad you found me and told me."

"Why wouldn't I have?"

"Not to speak ill of the dead, but considering your sister's reputation, I'm surprised you weren't concerned I'd be just like her."

"Honestly?"

"Of course," he smiles.

I look dead into his eyes so he can see I'm telling the truth. I swallow deeply, getting captivated by his eyes. God they're beautiful. Shaking my head of my thoughts I begin. "At first I didn't want to find you. I wondered about everything going on in your life and if you were still doing the job that you do. I didn't want Imogen getting caught up in that. I've seen Die Hard and other movies when their kids get used for revenge. But I realised I was just making excuses. I guess in the end I just wanted what was best for her. I imagined what my life would be like without her and it killed me. Then I wondered what it would be like for you. I know you didn't know her, but she's special, she's a fighter, and she deserves the best of everything. You deserved to know her."

"WOW! Didn't expect you to be that honest."

"I just don't want hidden secrets. We've got to get along for Imogen. We need to talk about everything. I know nothing about you, vice versa."

"We'll get there, I promise, but first, let's get Immy to bed and talk about what happened this morning, okay?" he says bumping my chin with his fist. I look into his eyes, giving him a watery smile. I've never had anyone give me what he's giving me right now. What happened this morning has honestly scared me the loving poop out of me. I don't want to be one of those scared women, but I know if it hadn't been for Evan taking us in, I would still be at home scared at my wits end.

"Okay," I nod and take care of Imogen. I lay her down in the new comfy cot and wrap her up snugly, but not too snug that she'll overheat. The nights are getting colder as of late but, thankfully, Evan can afford to have his heating on, unlike me. It's not a luxury I was used to having.

It's another reason it's going to kill me when it's time for me to finally leave here. I don't want to leave Imogen, she's my life, but looking at what Evan could give her in a day has me wondering if she's better off without me.

SEVEN

EVAN

I HAD TO GET OUT OF THERE. The room was suffocating me, and with her wearing my t-shirt and the image of her body from earlier still haunting me, I couldn't handle being so close. I've never had a woman affect me the way she does.

I was glad she'd been dead to the world when I got her undressed because I would have hated her seeing my reaction. First it was the desire that had hit me hard seeing her so vulnerable, so peaceful. Her face had been relaxed, free of any turmoil she had going on inside that head of hers. But then I had seen the bruises that fucker had inflicted on her. I had to go outside and kick the shit out of the dustbin to get my frustration out. I fucking hate men that lay their hands on women. It's weak, insulting to other men, and down straight wrong.

Don't get me wrong, I've seen women hit men and even been in situations where I've had to restrain a woman from hurting their bloke. But still, men that prey on weaker, innocent women, or any women, infuriate me, and by the look of Kennedy's bruises she had no chance in hell of fighting back. The bloke that did it didn't hold back. She's such a tiny, delicate thing that it's hard picturing someone wanting to hurt her.

Walking into the kitchen I take the containers from out of the microwave and place them on the side. Getting a couple of fresh plates out, I start grabbing some stuff for myself when Kennedy walks in.

"Smells yummy."

See? So fucking cute.

"Here, take what you like. I'll warm it up for you. I ordered it an hour or so ago."

"What time is it?" she asks looking around for a clock.

"It's just gone eleven."

"Oh gosh! I can't believe I slept that long," she gasps, grabbing food. I'm actually surprised she's throwing food on her plate the way she is. She doesn't seem like the type of person that would stuff her face in front of a male. Then again, we aren't dating. Every other girl that I've dated has eaten like they're worried someone will notice. It pissed me off. Everyone eats to survive, it's not like what they're doing is rare.

"Like I said, you must have needed it," I tell her smiling. Walking into the front room after I've finished heating up our food, she follows me.

"I just feel bad. I mean, I left Imogen with you and you've only just met each other. Then I crash in your bed like I own the place. It just doesn't feel right. Me being here and all."

"I wouldn't have offered, Kennedy, if I didn't mean it. I want to help you and having you here will help keep you safe. I'm not going to let you get hurt. Again."

In fact, having her here feels right somehow and not just because of Imogen either. Something about seeing her lay in my bed sleeping did something to me. But I know with everything going on, if I start something with her it will most likely end badly.

"Thank you," she whispers, and by the way she's staring down at her plate I would imagine she doesn't have this kind of help all the time.

"What do you do for a living?" I ask her, wanting to get to know her.

She looks up from her plate and when she finishes chewing she looks at me nervously. "I work in a cafe in town. I'm hoping to get something better, but there aren't many jobs going."

She's cute when she rambles.

"How long have you been working there?"

"Four years," she tells me hesitantly. "What about you, how long have you een working for the police?"

"I'm not working for them now. I've actually started my own business with a good friend of mine, Harris."

"Sounds interesting. What will you be doing now?" she asks, taking another bite from her food.

"A bit of everything, I guess. We will be fitting security systems for people, private investigations and security for people that hire us. It will vary. We'll still have to look into cheating spouses, but it will get better."

"Sounds really good. If you don't mind me asking, what happened with my sister? The night, you know, Imogen was conceived. Even though I know she was a b.i.t.c.h. I never thought she'd be capable of that," she tells me, whispering when she spells the word bitch.

Then it occurs to me. I've never heard her swear. I chuckle and she gives me a strange look which only makes me grin.

Putting the plate down, finished with my food, I look to Kennedy with a serious expression. "I'm not really supposed to talk about the case or anything involved with it, but because no harm can really come of it, I'll tell you. Your sister was mixed up with some pretty shitty people. I had been undercover for a year. Your sister had always come on to me, but I always pushed her away. And before you ask, it wasn't because I was on a job; it was because I didn't like your sister. I know that's wrong, she's your sister and all, but..."

"I understand, you don't need to apologise, she has never been the nicest girl so whatever you have to say I can take it."

I give her a gentle smile and store that information in the back of my mind for later. I want to know how the two of them could be complete opposites.

"Well, she basically sold herself to the men if they offered and slept with the ones she thought she could get something out of. She hung around the unit more than any of the men who worked there.

"I guess on the last night, before the whole raid happened, she thought she would slip me something, though I can never prove that. I hadn't drunk anything until that night. I wanted to keep a level head, but my boss said I needed to make sure that I blended in, that I needed to be relaxed.

"I started to feel funny, light-headed, and my vision turned blurry. The next thing I knew I woke up naked in one of the bunks at the back of the unit with your sister next to me. Every day afterwards I would remember something else about that night, about her," I tell her, keeping my voice indifferent. I don't want her to really know how much it bothered me knowing my dick had been inside her skanky sister.

"Oh my, gosh," she gasps, her eyes watering. "I can't believe her. Did you know she was pregnant?"

"What? No! Why do you ask?"

"Because she told me she told you, but some stuff got in the way."

"No. If I had known I would have taken Imogen far, far away from her," I promise her, and she gives me a small smile.

"She left the night she gave birth," she blurts out, and I feel my eyes go wide. "What?"

"Yeah. She didn't care. After a week the hospital helped me get parental guardianship of Imogen so I could grant permission for the tests they needed to do. I found Vicky, got her to sign away her rights. I got granted full custody when Vicky died."

"How are you two totally different?" I ask out loud and watch a faint pink blush rise on her cheeks.

"I don't know," she whispers. "She was always like it. Even as a kid. I'm the youngest, my brother, who died from cot death when he was six months old, would have been the eldest. My mom always put her attitude down to being the middle child, but I always saw something dark within her, you know?"

"She was always getting into trouble, even before everything happened. When our parents died she got worse. We got separated for a while before they found us a home to take us both in, but even then she ruined it. In the end they put me with a good family, one that agreed to still let me see her, but not live with her. She resented me for that, I think."

"You didn't get along?" I ask her. I'm not surprised to hear any of this. I knew Vicky had a hard past and that her parents died. I also knew she had a sister, but she was never checked out with the investigation. But I guess I always presumed she was just like her. I couldn't have been more wrong.

"Not from the first time I can remember. She'd take everything my parents ever bought me. Whether it was a pair of knickers that would never have fitted her, she'd take it. She caused arguments, fights and never cared who she was hurting. She'd bully me non-stop," she shrugs.

Jesus. Her sister really was a fucking bitch. And to grow up with her as her only family must have sucked.

At least now she has me and Imogen.

Fuck! Where the hell did that come from? Needing a drink I get up quickly, startling her. "I'm going to get a beer. Do you want one or do you want something else?" I ask taking her empty plate.

"Um, I'll have a water, or tea, thanks," she smiles, sitting back in the chair. She looks so lost and small in that chair. It completely swallows her tiny frame.

Walking back in I hand Kennedy her tea and take my seat back on the sofa. Kennedy has made herself at home and has tucked her feet under her and got a pillow snuggled on her belly with her cup of steaming hot tea in her hand.

"So," I start. Picking up the files I move closer towards her. "I've been going through these files all night and so far I can't pick anything up from what you told me. I've had a folder of pictures brought over of everyone connected to the case. Can you take a look and see if you recognise him?"

She nods her head firmly, but with the way her hands shake I can tell she is remembering everything from this morning and is nervous as hell.

"Are you doing okay?" I ask as she flicks through them.

"I guess. Everything seems to have happened so quickly. My whole body feels swollen and it aches. But other than the fact I don't understand what is going on, I'm fine."

"I promise he won't touch you again," I tell her strongly, needing her to hear the truth in my words.

She looks up from the folder and holds my eye contact. "I know you won't."

The way she says it has my heart beating overdrive. She's putting her trust in me so willingly and she doesn't even know me. But I can't help but feel a sense of pride at hearing her put so much faith in me. She didn't even question herself.

Not knowing what else to say I let her flick through the folder in silence. Meanwhile, I keep myself busy and flick through tonight's highlights of the game that I missed.

Half an hour later I hear a squeak come from Kennedy. Turning towards her I find tears running down her face, her hand over her mouth, and her eyes wide with fear and recognition.

"Have you found him?" I ask, kneeling down in front of her and taking both her hands in mine. "Look at me."

"It's him," she whispers. Removing her one hand from my grasp she points down at a picture. I take the folder from her and look at the picture in front of me.

"Fuck!"

"What?" she asks panicked. I sit back on my heels and run a hand through my hair.

Damon fucking White. One of the biggest, most ruthless drug suppliers in town. No one has ever been able to get that fucker charged with anything. Even with the evidence we had stacked against him he still got let off.

"Tell me! You're scaring me," Kennedy pleads and I snap my head up to hers. Seeing her look so scared has me wanting to pull her into my arms.

"Are you sure this is him?" I ask quietly.

"Yes. I'll never forget those eyes or that scar," she tells me. Her body is shaking uncontrollably and she's starting to become hysterical.

"Look, everything is going to be okay, but this guy? This guy is seriously bad news. Whatever your sister was mixed up in with him is bad. He's not known to give second chances. He also demands having a backup plan for people who buy off him."

"That's why he threatened me to pay up or he'd take Imogen," she hiccups, tears falling down her face. I wipe them away, but they keep on flowing. Seeing her like this is breaking my heart.

"Babe, he won't touch you again," I promise her. I grab my phone off the table and dial William's number.

"You better have a reason for interrupting my television time," he growls and any other time I'd tease him, but this is serious.

"I need that help you promised me," I tell him in a serious voice.

"Fuck! Who is it?"

"Damon White."

"Shit!"

EIGHT

KENNEDY

TOSSING AND TURNING LAST NIGHT kept me up after hearing the way Evan talked to his old boss on the phone. He tried not to look worried, but I could see it in his eyes.

The way he tried to comfort me last night still flashes through my mind. I can still feel his soft fingers running across my cheeks, wiping away my tears and the way he held my hands. The way his voice would carry a certain gentleness to it but still sound so sure and firm at the same time.

I'm not looking forward to today and when I say that, I honestly mean it. I don't know what's going to happen.

Evan told me they've put a warrant out for this Damon guy's arrest but, with no witnesses, his lawyer will have him out in no time. I asked why he was bothering getting him arrested if it wasn't going to happen. He explained that he wanted to spook Damon, to let him know that they're watching him in the hope that it gets him to back off. Personally, I don't think he truly believes himself that he will. He couldn't even look me in the eye when he said it to me.

After feeding Imogen and getting her dressed I put her in her Bumbo activity floor seat and made Evan breakfast. I felt bad that he had to sleep on his sofa. Even though it's big, with his large frame it must have been uncomfortable for him.

A knock at the door startles me from what I'm doing. I drop the dishcloth and move to the hall to see if Evan heard. After he had eaten he went to get showered and dressed. Still hearing the shower, I walk towards the door, hoping it's just the postman or a sale marketer.

"Hey...Oh hi, um...is...is Evan here?" a beautiful woman asks. I remember seeing her the first time I visited. She lives next door, I think.

I blush when the thought of her being Evan's girlfriend enters my mind. Sugar! Does she know about Imogen? Or me? Or why we're here? Will she go crazy on me?

"Yes, he's...um...he's in the shower. Would you like to come in and wait?"

Before she answers Imogen starts crying wildly from her Bumbo seat and I rush off leaving the door wide open so I can go to her.

I hear the woman walk inside and when I turn I notice she's left the door open behind her.

"If he's busy I can come back," she tells me sadly, not looking at me. Have I made things awkward?

Sugar! Did they break up over Imogen?

"He'll be out..."

"Oh, hey, Lexi. I thought I heard the door," he says and I turn and nearly choke on my own saliva. Wet, tanned and tattooed, Evan stands in only a towel. A tribal tattoo runs from his chest and down his ribs. Another tattoo of a dragon covers the top half of his arm. How did I not know he had tattoos? How did I miss them?

What has me squeezing my thighs together and taking a large gulp is his abdomen. It's lean, sculpted and drool worthy. Each muscle is defined by deep ridges, and I yearn to run my fingers down them.

He catches me staring and his eyes turn darker. I spin around to avoid his intense stare, rocking a crying Imogen in my arms.

"I wanted to talk to you, but I can see that this is a bad time," she says and turns to go, but Evan's deep rumbling voice stops her.

"Hold up. Let me just go get some clothes on and we'll talk," he tells her. He doesn't give her a chance to answer, leaving no room for argument which I've found in the day I've known him, he does a lot. He rushes back down the hall to his bedroom, leaving me standing here feeling awkward.

"I'm Kennedy," I introduce myself, manoeuvring Imogen to my other arm so I can reach out to shake hers.

"I'm Lexi," she smiles but it doesn't reach her eyes. She shakes my hand and let's go quickly, taking a step back. Trying to calm Imogen down has made it hard to study Lexi, but from what I can tell she seems like a nice person. She doesn't come off as standoffish, even with her uncomfortable silence. One thing that is clear for me to see is that she doesn't like me being here.

"Would you like a drink?" Evan asks walking back in, now wearing jeans and a short sleeved black t-shirt.

"NO!" Lexi blurts out but then quietens her voice. "Sorry. No. I can't stay long," she smiles and frowns when Evan walks over towards me and holds his hands out for Imogen. I give him a smile, loving how easily he's taken to her already. He's a hands-on dad that's for sure.

"Okay. I'd like you to meet someone, this is Kennedy," he starts, and Lexi smiles.

"We've met."

"And this little pumpkin is, Immy, short for Imogen. She's my daughter," he smiles proudly. He's so busy gazing down at a fussy Imogen that he doesn't notice the way Lexi's face falls. I want to reach out and comfort her, but something about her body language and expression has me staying out.

"Daughter?" she chokes out. The way she says 'daughter' has my blood pumping. It's like the word sounded bitter in her mouth.

The tone of her voice has Evan looking up and frowning at Lexi in confusion.

"Hey, she's my daughter."

"Oh, fuck! I forgot I have a doctor's appointment. I best be going before I'm late," she states quickly. I want to snap at her for swearing around a baby, but most of all for swearing. It's one thing that drives me insane. Women that swear make themselves sound really trashy. I know I don't have room to judge, it's just a pet peeve of mine and women who look like Lexi shouldn't use that kind of language. It makes her sound common.

I watch as Evan opens his mouth and move towards her, but Lexi is out of the door before he can take another step. I watch like a deer caught in headlights and wonder what I should do.

"Do you want me to take Imogen so you can go after her?" I ask quietly, feeling bad it's mine and Imogen's presence that has caused this.

"Why?" He asks so simply I begin to wonder if he's really qualified to be a cop. He should already know why. It doesn't take a genius to work out what was going on with her.

"Because I don't want you two to break up," I start, but Evan's laughter interrupts me. "What?" I frown, not liking the fact he's laughing at me.

"You think we're together?" he asks sounding amused.

"She's in love with you, that's clear to see and when I opened the door she looked like her whole world had fallen apart," I tell him.

"Look, I know she was lying about the doctor's appointment. I just don't know why. But I can assure you that we have never been together."

"Why do I have a feeling there's a *but*?" I ask but then shake my head embarrassed. "I'm sorry, it's none of my business."

His eyes soften and he takes a step closer towards me. "You're going to be in my life for a long time, Kennedy. You deserve to know."

"Okay," I whisper, trying to ignore the way his words are doing crazy things to my insides right now.

"I thought we had a thing a while back, but it was nothing. In fact, *she* turned *me* down."

"But you're hot!" I shout, outraged, then end up groaning. I need a flipping filter. Why do I always do this to myself? It doesn't help that he's so good looking. It makes me more on edge than normal.

"Thanks, so are you," he winks and it makes me blush. "It took me a while to realise that it would never have worked out between us. I was hoping for something that wasn't there between us."

"What do you mean?" I ask curiously, grinning when I see Imogen lying down on Evan's shoulder, her mouth hanging open in an O shape, sleeping.

"I want to settle down. A lot had happened last year with my sister and when I was told she had a baby, and a fiancé, I realised what I had been missing," he shrugs but I can see it still matters to him. He still wants that.

"You sure it's not some sibling rivalry?" I tease.

He chuckles, the sound sending shivers up my spine. "No. I love my sister and would give her the world if I could because she deserves it. But seeing it there, right in front of me, just hit me. I wanted to be settled down in a family home and not some three bed bungalow. And someday have it filled with kids."

"You got one of those," I remind him, smiling at a snoring Imogen.

"Yeah, I do don't I," he smiles but when I look up at him, he's smiling at me and the look in his eyes is something I've never seen before.

"So...um... was there something you needed to do today before you have to be in the station?" I ask. My stomach has been turning violently since he told me he'd have to leave us today to go in when they've arrested Damon. He said he wanted to be there to see for himself what happens and what Damon's reaction will be. Luckily, his old boss is okay with him doing that as long as he doesn't cause a scene.

"Funny you should ask that. Everything that had happened with my sister last year caused her to fall out with me as such. Her boyfriend just texted me to tell me she's over her snit and to come over whenever to visit. Now that I know Immy is really mine I was wondering if we could go see her. I want her to be the first person to meet her."

I pause for a second thinking about it. I've never really left Imogen with anyone other than the nursery staff and on the odd occasion, Melanie. Sucking it up I give Evan a smile.

"Sure. I'll do some washing and stuff. Clean up the mess Imogen and I have made. It's the least I could do for you letting us stay."

"No, Kennedy, you don't understand. I want you to come as well."

"To meet your sister?" I ask, my voice high pitched.

"Yes," he chuckles, but I give him a glare.

"I can't meet your sister. She might hate me or get the wrong idea. My sister was a... you know, and your sister might think I'm a... you know, too."

"No one would ever accuse you of being a bitch," he tells me softly and my eyes meet his and soften. My whole body sags and I find myself nodding when inside I'm shaking my head 'no'. Meeting the family? Not high on my list of things to do. People hear about where I came from, who I'm related to and they judge me. They judge me for what my sister has done and as soon as Denny finds out what my sister did to her brother she's going to hate me. There's no way that she won't.

"Okay...But don't leave me," I add on quickly, really not wanting to be left alone. I don't know anything about his family or what they're like.

Jeeze Louise, it's his sister, how hard can it be?

Turns out it's harder than I imagined.

NINE

EVAN

Knocking on my sister's door I begin to feel nervous as fuck. I'm not a nervous kind of guy. I'm always so calm and collected. Fuck, it's my job to say calm and on alert. But until now I didn't realise how much I want my sisters blessing, her approval. I know she'll be pissed once she finds out about Vicky but I want her to accept Kennedy and Imogen into our lives.

"Alright, mate. She's just getting Hope dressed," Mason tells us opening the door wider. He looks at Kennedy curiously then down at Imogen. I notice his head snapping quickly in my direction and it makes me wonder if he has clicked on to Imogen being mine. Now that I've had time to really look at Immy I can see myself in her.

"Thanks," I nod.

We follow him into the front room where I drop the car seat down by the single arm chair, signalling to Kennedy to sit down. She's been strangely quiet from the moment I told her she was coming with us. I don't know why but her not being with me had me feeling unsettled. It didn't feel right letting the family meet Immy and not her. It's like she belongs at my side.

Footsteps from the stairs have me standing back up from the sofa. When Denny walks in she looks surprised to see me, but more surprised and curious as to who Kennedy is. She gives Imogen a quick glance and I ignore the pang of disappointment in my chest at her not seeing Imogen is mine the way Mason did.

"Hey," she greets slowly, handing a happy Hope over to Mason.

"Hey, sis," I smile then move forward to wrap her up in a hug. "I'm sorry, for everything," I whisper in her ear.

"It's not your fault. I was just too stubborn to see that."

I shake my head ready to argue but then her head tilts in Kennedy's direction. Shit. Here it goes.

"This is Kennedy and this little one is Imogen, my daughter."

She doesn't say anything for a second and I start to worry. My sister has an opinion on everything and anything.

"Excuse me?"

"I didn't know about her, not until a month ago, but then we were waiting for the DNA results to come back," I breathe out.

"DNA results? I don't understand. How did this happen?"

"I'm pretty certain you should know that," I tease lightly, trying to ease the mood.

"But, I didn't think you were seeing anyone. You said you didn't have time..." she begins and I can see where she's going with this. After everything that happened when she was kidnapped I explained to her that I never had time to do anything. Which was true. I never had time to get laid, let alone visit family.

"It's a long story. I was drugged, taken advantage of, and didn't find out about Imogen until a month ago," I start, rubbing my face. I can't believe I'm having to explain this to my sister. I wanted more time before I had to talk about the deep stuff.

"Are you fucking kidding me? You bring a slut into my house, near my kid. GET OUT," Denny shouts at Kennedy, she stands up, her eyes watering, her body visibly shaking.

"What?" I ask looking between them, wondering why she's having such a strong outburst towards Kennedy. Kennedy's eyes fill with tears and like I do it every day, I walk over to her and wrap my arms around her shoulders. She tries to push me off but I don't let her.

"Watch your mouth, Denny," I snap and watch Mason move to put Hope in her bouncy chair.

"Are you serious right now, Evan? She raped you, she assaulted you and kept your baby away from you," she snaps looking between me and Kennedy.

"Denny," I begin, cursing to myself. "Kennedy isn't Imogen's biological mother. Imogen has been left in Kennedy's care. She's Imogen's biological mother's, sister."

She pauses, tears filling her own eyes. "What?"

"She's not the person who did what you're accusing," I state, not wanting to use the term rape.

"You just let me speak to her like that," she gasps.

"I didn't think. Fucking hell, I'm nervous as fuck here. It's not every day you find out you're a dad and then move the mom and kid in," I tell her, waving my hands in the air. Honestly it feels good to get all this shit out.

"You moved her in?" Denny breathes but her eyes narrow at the last minute. "Are you sure about all of this? How do you know she's not using you?"

Her attitude is starting to piss me off. "You're seriously going to go there? As I recall you and Mason didn't have the best start. At least when Kennedy found me she didn't mess around to tell me I'm Imogen's dad," I snap, feeling my blood boil. How dare she?

Her eyes go wide. Mason steps forward, his posture rigid, itching to fight. "I think you should go," he growls and my eyes narrow on his.

"Don't worry, I am," I snap back then look to my sister. "I wanted you to be the first to know, the first to meet her, but I was wrong. Out of everyone I never expected you to react like this. If you can't accept Kennedy and Imogen into your life, into mine, then I don't want to know. You can be the one to explain to Hope why she doesn't see her cousin and her uncle," I snap, grabbing the car seat and Kennedy's hand. I don't bother stopping to console Denny when I hear her cry or when Mason growls something at me. I just keep walking.

"Hey, mate," one of Mason's brothers calls walking towards Mason's. When he sees my facial expression he frowns, but doesn't say anything further. I'm glad he doesn't because I'm ready to blow a fuse. After getting Imogen strapped into the car, I move around to the passenger side of the car, opening the door for Kennedy. Once she's in I start to buckle her in like a dickhead, but her hand reaching for mine stops me. My head snaps up looking into her dark brown, sad eyes. They're filled with tears and I know she's struggling to hold them back.

Not able to prevent what I was about to do, my hands reach out to her cheeks, my thumbs running lightly under her eyes as the first of her tears fall. We stare into each other's eyes, neither one of us able to find the strength to look away. The dead silence in the air becomes too much and I find myself blinking, moving my hands away from her face.

Whatever just passed between us is something neither one of us is ready for.

Driving in silence starts to get to me after five minutes into the drive. I'm about to break the silence when Kennedy's sweet, small voice carries across the car.

"I'm sorry, so sorry." A soft sob escapes her mouth and I reach across the console, grabbing her hand in mine, wondering what's wrong. It's cold under my warm touch and I see her shiver from the corner of my eye. What's puzzling is the fact she feels the need to say sorry. She isn't in the wrong. I shouldn't have taken either of them. I should have spoken to Denny on my own first and explained everything, not just dump it on her all at once.

"No, I'm sorry. I didn't know she would be that judgemental. I should have explained over the phone or gone on my own to see her first. I shouldn't have subjected you to that."

"I don't want you to fall out with your family," she whispers. "Not over me, not over what my sister did. Imogen doesn't deserve it."

"Hey," I say softly, squeezing her hand with mine. "You're right. She doesn't deserve this; she deserves a family that accepts her for who she is and not where she came from or how she was conceived. As much as I hated what Vicky did, I have Imogen. I have you," I tell her, the last part more of a whisper. Her intake of breath tells me she has heard me, but something inside me can't bring myself to care. It's the truth. There is just something about her that has me feeling overprotective, that wants to get to know her. It's not just about her looks, because she is hot as fuck. But it's the way she loves and adores Imogen. It's the way she willingly put Imogen first, even though it meant she'd be in danger. She's also incredibly sweet. She doesn't swear and the way she looks at me. Fuck! Just remembering the way she looked at me when I walked out in just a towel this morning makes my dick twitch. I wanted to bend her over the sofa and take her right there.

"I know. I just feel like this is my fault somehow. But then, no matter how I look at it, I'd have always turned up at your door and told you about Imogen."

"And you'll never truly understand how thankful I am to you for that. You'll also never understand how glad I am that you are who you are."

Kennedy laughs, catching me off guard, and I can't help but smile listening to her. It's the first time I've seen her laugh and her face... God, she's fucking beautiful.

"You really mean to say you're glad I'm not like my sister."

"There is that too," I laugh agreeing. "But seriously, I'm just glad it's you that will be the mother to my child," I admit, pulling up outside my house.

I stop the car, getting out and leaving Kennedy speechless. I walk around the car just as Lexi walks out of her house with the same date I'd seen her with the last time. When she sees me she gives me a small smile before laughing loudly at something her date says. I ignore them, and open Kennedy's door, kneeling down to talk to her.

"Are you okay?"

"You want me to be her mother?" she asks and when she turns her face is soaked from the heavy tears falling from her eyes.

"No, baby, you already are her mother," I tell her honestly.

She lets out a sob before throwing herself into my arms. I'm glad she had been able to take the seatbelt off before she did, otherwise she'd most likely have hurt her bruises.

She clings to my t-shirt sobbing, her tears soaking through the material. I rub her back and tell her that it's going to be okay. When she looks up her face is close to mine.

Everything freezes around us and it's just us in that moment. I lean in a touch to gauge her reaction. When she doesn't move away I take that as my cue and press my lips to hers. They're soft, full and I can't get enough. It's when I feel her tongue run along my bottom lip that everything in that moment switches, and instead of the slow, soft kiss, it becomes heated and aggressive. I can't hold her close enough. She moans into my mouth and I groan loudly, the zipper of my jeans digging into my erection.

A loud cry fills the car and snaps us both out of our embrace. The lust and desire I was feeling a minute ago evaporates a little.

We turn our heads slightly to Imogen as if just realising she's in the car, that she's a major factor in our relationship, before turning back to each other. I open my mouth, but nothing comes out. Her whole face is pale which has her full lips looking fuller and redder. Her tears have now dried, but her eyes still shine with tears.

She's beautiful.

I get up not knowing what to say. I cough once, twice, before I find the courage to say something and when I do, "I'll get Immy," is the first thing that leaves my mouth. I inwardly groan at how stupid I sound. I'm a grown ass man who has no trouble talking to a room full of people, making new friends or any of that bullshit. I've never had a problem picking up girls, in fact, they usually flock to me, but with Kennedy, I find everything I've learnt from experience has been erased from my memory. It's like everything is new with her, including the feelings she evokes in me.

She nods her head and I move out of the way making my way to the back driver's side to get Imogen out. When I do my eyes reach Lexi's and the look of hurt from meeting my sister is still written all over her expression. I'm not even a little bit sorry I spoke to my sister like that. I needed her to know Kennedy and Imogen are now in my life.

Opening the door, Imogen's fussing in her seat and pulling at her ears when I look down at her. My eyes snap to Kennedy's with concern and her face turns pale.

"What's wrong?" she asks, rushing around the car.

"She was doing that this morning," I tell her when she notices the same thing.

"Yeah, the doctors said she's teething. Everything I've read on it says the same thing, but it still worries me," she tells me, moving me aside to unbuckle Imogen.

"Here, I got her," I tell her, moving her out of the way, my one hand on her hip. She stiffens under my touch and testing the waters I press myself against her, loving the feel of her backside pressed up against me. She melts into my body like butter and I can't help but smirk at the fact.

After a second or two of enjoying her pressed against me, Imogen once again starts to cry and we both move to the left to let each other past, only, we end up bumping into each other. We do the same again, only this time we both move to the right. Chuckling, I grab a hold of Kennedy's hips and pick her up, turning and placing her down behind me like she weighs nothing. Her eyes are wide and filled with desire and her luscious mouth is open in shock.

I grab Imogen and her changing bag from the back of the car before locking up and walking towards the house. Kennedy already has the spare key ready and is opening the door when I get there.

I watch her ass swing side to side in her tight ass jeans and will myself not to get another hard on with my daughter in my arms. I look up walking in and pray like hell that I can get through the night without pouncing on her and taking her, making her fully mine. Now that I've had a taste my body is already craving more of her.

The minute the door shuts behind me my phone starts ringing in my back pocket. Grabbing it, I look at the screen and groan.

She couldn't keep her mouth shut.

"Hey, Nan," I answer, not able to hide my discomfort.

"You got something to tell me, young man?"

"I cannot believe she had the nerve to call you. I wanted to tell you myself."

"She called me in absolute tears. Now, I want to hear it from you," she says sternly, not a tone I'm used to my nan using with me.

"Long story short, on my last job, before Denny's case, I was drugged and used. Just over a month ago, the sister of the woman who used me came knocking on my door to me tell me about Imogen, my five month old baby. I didn't believe it at first, but she came with a DNA test. We sent it off and wham bam, the baby's mine. They're both living with me, and the biological mom is dead," I rush out, hating that I'm repeating myself. I've still got my dad to tell but I know Denny has probably called him by now too. The thought angers me. She knew I would want to tell the others but after her reaction I was going to put it off until she calmed down.

"Oh my, sweetie. You were raped," she gasps and I hear tears in her voice.

"No, Nan. I don't look at it like that. Yes, I was taken advantage of, but I don't feel like a victim," I tell her, looking at Kennedy and rolling my eyes. She gives me a small smile before settling down on the sofa with Imogen and a fresh bottle. I feel like shit that she's the one feeding her. She needs a break. She still looks tired, worn and sore as fuck from the attack. Even after sleeping most of the day yesterday.

"Are you listening to me?" my nan snaps, causing my body to jolt.

"Sorry, I um... look, I need to go I have another call," I lie.

"I'm coming round in the week. Don't think of making excuses. I'll come when you're least expecting it," she warns. Yeah, she'll most likely turn up at five in the morning just so we don't escape or make up a lame ass excuse.

"Okay, love you," I tell her.

"Love you too and Evan?"

"Yeah?"

"I can't wait to meet Imogen," she says softly. A smile breaks out across my face at having her approval. She ends the call and I look down at the phone, still smiling. Only my nan could make me smile when I'm still feeling angry over Denny and the shit that came out of her mouth.

When my phone rings again I think it's my nan again, but when I look down at the phone it's William and my heart stops.

"Yeah?"

"You need to come in, now!" is all he says before ending the call. My eyes immediately look to Kennedy. She's here and she's safe. But the feeling in the pit of my stomach has me twisted up inside giving me a bad feeling about all this Damon business.

TEN

KENNEDY

THE HOUSE IS QUIET NOW that Imogen has gone down for a nap and Evan has gone to the station to sort out all this business my sister has me involved in. I won't lie; I'm scared out of my mind. Scared that this is going to make things worse for me and Imogen, but then I realise nothing could be worse than him taking her from me. Whoever Damon White is it's definitely clear he's bad news and if Evan is worried, then I'm terrified. He doesn't seem like the person who gets worried over nothing. He's strong, good looking and a fantastic kisser. He's also incredibly attentive to Imogen and has been generous and kind towards me. Did I mention he's a great kisser?

Holy-amaze-balls he is such a good kisser. I can still feel him on my lips. It's amazing that in one moment, one kiss, my whole world can change in an instant. I knew then and there that Evan meant something to me, more than my niece, no, daughter's father.

I'm still in shock over the whole conversation we had earlier out by his car. His words, the meaning behind them, will forever be embedded in my memory. For him to think of me already as her mom is just.... Let's just say, I've never felt so overwhelmed in all my life. I'm ecstatic and want to scream 'she's mine' from the top of my lungs, but then on the other hand I want to hide in Evan's room and cry until the sun comes up in the morning. Everything just seems to be happening so quickly and it's terrifying me.

My life was boring before Vicky turned up pregnant. We hardly spoke with each other before. The only time she'd answer my calls or call me herself is when she was in trouble and needed my help. I'd never give her money. I knew where it would go. I didn't want to be a part of her killing herself.

I cook me and Evan some dinner while I wait for him. When he doesn't turn up at six like he said he would I start to eat by myself, but my appetite seems lost with worrying about him.

It's half eight when the door finally opens and he walks in looking grim and worse for wear. I immediately sit up from the sofa where I've been lounging for the past hour watching some soaps.

"Is everything okay?" I ask, my heart beating fast. The look he gives me tells me all I need to know. This isn't going to be good news.

"I've got something I need to tell you," he says grimly, sitting down on the sofa next to me.

"Oh, no! What is it? What happened?"

"Damon got let out. He has an alibi that the police checked out and without any further evidence they can't keep him."

"Oh my gosh. What is going to happen? I didn't lie to you, Evan. It was him," I cry, feeling tears sting my cheeks. I've had it with crying. It's all I seem to do lately.

"Hey, babe, I know you're not lying. The police know you're telling the truth, but Damon, he's conniving. He knows how to manipulate everyone around him. He has always managed to stay one step ahead of the police. I think he knew you would go to the police."

"So, what happens now? I wait around for him to do something to me, to Imogen?" I cry. "Could today get any worse," I sob into my hands.

"Um, yeah, it can. That's not all I needed to talk to you about. I may or may not have gone postal on his ass, and he knows you're here, with me."

My head flies up to Evan and I gasp. He looks apologetic and I know he's sincere, but I have to get Imogen somewhere safe.

"I need to get Imogen safe. He can do what he likes to me but I can't risk Imogen, Evan," I tell him frantically. I stand up ready to go, but he pulls me back down and I land on his lap. At first it doesn't register, I'm too busy having a panic attack over this Damon guy and getting Imogen safe. So when I feel him harden underneath me I squirm, my breaths coming in short, fast pants. "Oh gosh," I whisper, but it comes out as a moan.

Evan makes a noise at the back of his throat, the sound sending a tingle between my legs. It's been so long since I've been with anyone sexually. Having him this close, this turned on, is doing nothing to keep my mind focused.

"I'm not going to let him hurt you or Imogen. I think he knows that and will hopefully back off. He should know by now not to fuck with anyone on my team," he says with conviction.

I turn, looking into his beautiful eyes. "But what if you can't? I honestly don't care what happens to me, but if anything happened to Imogen, I'd never be able to live with myself."

His face moves closer, his breath fanning across my face causing my breath to hitch. "I don't know what the future holds, Kennedy, but you and Immy, you have already come to mean something to me. You might not care what happens to you, but I do."

I sit on his lap stunned completely speechless. I've never had anyone talk to me like that, or tell me that they care for me the way he just did.

"We don't know each other," I whisper honestly. Although, I can't deny the fact, I feel like I've known him my whole life. The rugged, tattooed, handsome man has brought me to my knees. I shouldn't be so shocked. He caught my attention the second I laid eyes on him.

"We know enough, that's all that matters," he tells me, but then does something else that shocks me more, he kisses me. And just like earlier, my body sags into his embrace and clings onto him with a death grip. His lips are fuller than mine and cover them in a hard, deep kiss, his tongue sensually moving in sync with mine.

My body turns when his hands on my hips move me, and now instead of sitting across his lap, I'm straddling him, both legs bent on either side of him. He lies back against the couch and I follow, my lips never pulling away from his. It feels so good.

My hands move up to his strong, broad shoulders and I can't help but admire the strength and hardness as I do. He's built of stone, I swear. I already knew he was well defined in the muscle area, but to feel it with my own hands causes a flow of wetness to gather between my legs.

"We shouldn't be doing this," I mumble when I pull away, my eyes never moving from his swollen lips. They look inviting and I find myself moving closer, my lips yet again touching his. I can't get enough. I've never felt such satisfaction from just kissing someone, not that I've had a ton of experience, but the bit I do, kissing has always bored me. Until now.

My last boyfriend smoked and he tasted how I assume an astray would taste. That's how bad my experience with kissing is.

He pulls away, his eyes filled with desire and clouded over with lust as he looks to me. "This is a brilliant idea," he grins just before he moves in, capturing my lips again. His hands at my hips glide under my t-shirt, the rough pads of his finger tips run up against my ribs, until his thumbs are lightly touching underneath my breasts. My back arches into his touch, wanting him to pull down the cups of my bra to release the ache he's caused in my breasts.

Imagining him touching me so intimately causes a gush of wetness to leak from between my legs, and I begin to rub my sex against his hardness when the ache down there becomes too much to bear.

"We have Imogen to think about. If it goes wrong it could cause a rift between us," I tell him across his lips. He pulls away and I feel my shoulders sag. Even though I know he's doing right by Imogen, I can't help but feel the sadness that creeps in. We've not known each other long. Who sleeps with someone they barely know, but then I think about the people who have one night stands. I mean, most couples don't know each other when they first get together romantically, so what's saying they didn't start off just as fast at the beginning. Everyone has to start their relationship somewhere.

"Yes, we have Imogen and like I said to you earlier, I can't predict the future, but I can promise, no matter what, we'll both be in Imogen's life. You're thinking too hard. Just feel what you feel for me, Kennedy. Don't play what if, because I'll just throw some more back at you. What if this does happen and it happens because it was meant to be? What if it happens and everything works out for the best? There are always other choices to go along with, Kennedy, but I need you to make your choice and mean it. I'm hard as rock and have been since the moment you knocked on my door over a month ago," he grins, looking up at me.

I stare at him, shocked by his honesty. Who would have thought it, aye, Evan, wanting a girl like me. But it's more than that. He's willing to work at us. I can tell he means every word. The look in his eyes is pure honesty. And he's right. I could choose not to see where our attraction leads and lose what could be the best thing to ever happen to me, or I could lose myself in our attraction and end up with everything I've wanted.

I nod my head agreeing with him and I pray hard that I don't screw this up, whatever this is building between us. It's not like he actually mentioned a relationship, but I can't dwell on anything. My need for him is just rising with every brush of his fingers.

Kissing me deeply, I sigh into his mouth. I need more. Thinking we were going to move further than kissing, I'm surprised when Evan pulls away from me, looking at me with a soft expression. He kisses the tip of my nose before pulling back to look at me.

"How are you feeling?" he asks with concern.

"Horny," I blurt out, then groan, leaning forward and hiding my face in the crook of his neck. "I cannot believe I just said that out loud."

He's still chuckling when he lifts his hand, bumping my chin so I can look at him. "Don't ever be shy to tell me what's going on in your mind. But as much as I love that I'm turning you on," he chuckles, and my face heats. "I'm on about the whole Damon business."

"Oh..." I chuckle, feeling my cheeks flush red. "I guess I'm okay. I'm pissed and scared that he's going to get away with what he has done and I'll worry about what he's going to do next, but I also know there's nothing I can do. I don't have the money he wants no matter if I sold everything I own. All I can do is wait around and see what happens. If he's as bad as you say he is then hopefully he gets picked up for something else and gets put away for a long time."

"Just promise me that whatever you do, you keep an eye on everything around you. You've not been to work the past few days, so I'm guessing you have to go back soon."

"Oh, I have the week off. I thought I mentioned that to you," I tell him, thinking back to some of conversations, not able to pull up a memory of me telling him.

"Oh, so I have you to myself for a few more days? Want to do something with Immy? I know she's young but we'll take pictures so she can see them when she's older," he grins like a kid and I can't help but smile back. I nod my head 'yes', but before I have chance to do anything else, he grabs me by the hips and moves me so we're both lying down on our sides facing the television. "Now, let's watch something before Immy wakes up."

Silently, because I'm too stunned from being in such an intimate position, I grab the remote, clicking on the menu to see what's on. When I come across C.S.I. I click on the channel. Evan squeezes me on the hips, leans in and kisses me on the neck before leaning back against the couch.

It may seem weird to some, but lazing around and watching television like this with Evan could be my new favourite thing to do. His large body encircling my small frame makes me feel tiny, safe and protected. He feels like a giant wrapped around me. It's a feeling I could get used to after living on my own for years feeling scared of what will happen to me. The neighbourhood I live - lived - in wasn't the safest. It caused some anxiety over the years.

THREE DAYS LATER, with only one more day before I have to go back to work, there's another knock on the door.

I'm stunned for a second, worried why someone would willingly come out in this weather. It's been raining, thundering and lightning on and off the past two days. It's why we haven't been able to go out to the zoo as planned with Imogen. It had closed due to the weather.

Not that I'd take her out in this, she'd catch a death being out in it. It was freezing out there and the winds were terrible. Bins have blown over outside and rubbish is blowing all down the street.

Evan has popped to the shop to stock up on some nappies, wipes, and other essentials that we'll need for the next few days, so I don't have to go out in it.

The door knocks again and with Evan gone that leaves me to open the door, something I'm not overjoyed with doing after everything with Lexi.

When I open it a small woman with white hair is standing there with a handful of bags. She's getting soaked and I feel bad, but I don't know who she is.

"Um, can I help you?" I ask gently.

"My, aren't you a hot piece," she tells me, shocking me stunned. What on earth is going on? I look around for any hidden cameras, or maybe Damon. He could use this cute little old lady to lure me out, and it would work because I know I wouldn't say no to her. But her attitude? It makes me want to giggle. You'd never expect a woman her age to come out with such a blunt comment.

"Excuse me?" I ask over the pouring rain. Imogen starts to cry from her cot and I turn to the woman, torn about what to do. I don't want to shut the door on her in this weather. But like I said, I don't know who she is to just let her in.

"Is that my grandbaby?" she coos, pushing past me. The stacks of bags she's carrying hit me in the stomach where I'm still hurting from Damon's attack and I wince in pain.

"I'm sorry, but who are you?" Then I pause, her words hitting me like a truck. She's Evan's nan. Oh my gosh. And I didn't invite her in. How terrible of me. She's going to hate me more now, thinking I'm bad mannered.

"Let me just go get..." I start, but she drops her bags and turns to me.

"No, honey, you go and take a seat, put your feet up and I'll go get her. I bet my grandson has had you worn out in the bedroom," she winks before leaving me to stare at her back.

Did she just say what I think she said?

Oh my gosh! She thinks I'm sleeping with Evan. Good blimey. She thinks I'm a hussy. I straighten out my clothes and wish I made more of an effort this morning when I got dressed. I've just pulled on my leggings and my overlarge cream jumper that hangs off the one shoulder. My hair has been thrown up in a messy bun and I didn't bother with any makeup. I hardly wear it anyway.

Fiddlesticks.

She's even seen the bruises that are still clear on my face. Evan swore they'll fade soon enough, but they still look angry to me. The colour is the only thing that has changed. I'm just glad the swelling has gone down. It makes me feel somewhat better.

When I hear her talking to Imogen I snap out of my thoughts and rush across to the sofa. Evan and I were watching some movies and eating junk food before he went out, so all the wrappers are still scattered across the floor.

Quickly picking up the empty wrappers, I shove them in the empty Doritos packet. Then grab the empty glasses before taking them to the kitchen. I make it just in time for the lady to come down the hall carrying Imogen. I'm surprised she's stopped crying. She's been due a bottle for half an hour, but I didn't want to wake her. Plus, I've learnt in the time I've spent here that Evan loves feeding her. He loves doing everything in fact, but I see this look in his eyes whenever he thinks I'm not looking when I'm feeding her. He looks like he wants to tear her out of my arms, but mostly it's like he feels empty not having her in his arms. I laugh just thinking about it.

I quickly put the bottle in the hot boiling water to warm up when the front door knocks again. I look to the lady who I still don't know for sure is Evan's nan and smile.

"Can you watch her bottle for just a second, please?" I ask shyly.

"Of course," she smiles back and starts talking to Imogen about something.

Opening the door, I find Evan's next door neighbour standing under an umbrella. It's not the first time since the day she found out about Imogen that she's been over. In fact, if I was honest, I would think she was doing it on purpose.

"Um, hey," I smile, not sure what to say to her. She's always spoken to Evan when she's popped over, so I feel uncomfortable standing here.

"Is Evan here?" she asks, and she looks troubled which has me curious.

"No, he just popped out. Is there anything I can do?" I ask, then look down to find her wearing a dress of some kind. Not to sound like a B.I.T.C.H. but why on earth would you wear a dress in this weather? You'd be lucky not to catch a cold, let alone pneumonia.

"No. Can you tell him I need him to come around as soon as he's back please? It's an emergency," she asks kindly, and I smile nodding my head. When she turns I shout her name, calling her back. Instead of walking back, being polite, she just stops and turns, looking at me curiously.

"If it's an emergency are you sure I can't help? I'm sure there's something I can do?"

"Trust me, you can't," is all she replies before walking off.

"I'd watch your ass with that one. She's obviously trying to steal your man," the lady behind me says and I jump squealing.

"Sorry, you scared me. I'm Kennedy by the way," I tell her, introducing myself, hoping she'll return the favour.

"I'm Evan's, nan," she tells me and I groan inwardly. I can't call her Evan's nan. I need to know her name. I'm about to ask her what it is when she looks up from Imogen and smiles. "You can either call me Nan, or Mary. Both are fine with me."

"Nice to meet you, Mary," I beam, thanking God for answering my prayers. I shut the door behind me and move into the front room, following Mary.

"I don't want to sound rude, sweetie, you seem like a sweet girl and all, but are you using my Evan?"

"What? No! Why would you think that?" I ask, feeling my throat close up. Will all his family make assumptions about me just because of my sister?

"Because, honey, you have bruises on your face that tell me you're in trouble and it just seems too much of a coincidence that it happens to be the same time Evan finds out about Imogen."

"Oh... um... no! I'm not one to speak out of term but I feel like I need to get this out there," I tell her firmly. My hands are shaking but I clear my throat and move on. "When Imogen was born I didn't know anything about Evan, who he was, where he lived or anything. The only thing my sister said about him was that he was a rat and didn't want anything to do with the baby. I had no reason to doubt my sister," I half lie. Everything that came out of my sister's mouth I took with a pinch of salt. "It wasn't until my sister died that I found out his name and looked him up. As soon as I was free to, I sent him a letter. Imogen was still in the hospital so all my time was focused on her. I wrote more than once, never getting a reply. Then I turned up here. You know the rest. He done the DNA test for me, which, may I add, I paid for. When he turned up at my flat it was the day I was beaten, threatened and scared for not only Imogen's life, but my own. It seems my sister left me more than Imogen when she died and now I'm paying for a debt that she owed someone. If I don't pay then he's going to sell Imogen. That's the reason I'm here, and the only reason," I tell her, but even as the words leave my mouth I know they're a lie. Me being here may have started because I wanted to protect Imogen, but now I'm also staying to find out where this is going between me and Evan.

I really like him. And spending the last two days with him has only intensified that feeling.

"Well, I don't believe that's the only reason you're here," she winks and just like that, she throws me off guard again.

Seriously! She basically just accused me of being here for alternative reasons, but then when I explain, she answers with that? She's off her trolley.

Thankfully the door knocks again, but this time it's opened seconds after. I turn in my chair to see a soaking wet Evan walk in. I don't get any farther than that because I'm too busy staring at him. His black hair is dripping wet and droplets down his face, along his lips before falling to the floor. My eyes are captured by a single droplet that is dripping from his top lip. I have to fight the urge to go over to him and lick the droplets of rain from him. He's looking freaking hot and I can't help but stare.

He coughs, gaining my attention, and he gives me a smirk and a wink. He opens his mouth and I wait for him to say something sexy, to say anything, but then he turns and frowns at seeing his nan sitting down feeding Imogen.

"Nan, what are you doing here?" he asks her, but doesn't wait for a reply before turning back to me. "And I wanted to feed Immy," he pouts. Yes, fudging pouts. So darn cute.

"Well, Evan, it's nice to see you, too."

"And who's this?" he asks, pointing his thumb behind him. My eyes look behind him to find a man standing by the door looking sheepish. He's wearing a grin on his face, his eyes staring holes into Mary.

"We're sex buddies," she giggles and Evan groans covering his face with his hands.

I look open mouthed towards Mary to see if she's joking, but the look on her face as she eyes the gentlemen behind Evan tells me that she isn't.

I want to be sick for him. No people their age should have sex. It isn't right. I would hate to be Evan right now. She's his nan. But even so, I can't help the giggle that escapes my mouth. Evan sends me a warning look which causes me to smile.

"Please, Nan. Just....just don't talk about anything to do with other men."

"Well I only had a onetime fling with a woman, but I was too drunk to remember it, so I can't talk about women," she shrugs.

"Jesus. Fuck, Nan, tone it down before you scare poor Immy and Kennedy away."

"Alright. Now you can sit and tell me how you're going to help my girl," she demands all serious.

"What on earth are you on about?" he asks taking his jacket off and sitting down on the arm of my chair. I scoot over and he notices. Instead of sitting next to me, he slides down, lifts me up and places me over his lap. I'm shy at first. I mean, his fudging nan is right in front of us.

"Peter, come, darling, sit down," she tells him tapping the sofa. The man, who must be the same age as Mary, if not younger, sits down next to her and places his hand on her leg.

"Oi, hands to yourself," Evan barks causing Mary to giggle. I just stay quiet, fascinated by the whole thing. This is so weird and not at all like the families I grew up with.

Peter moves his hands with a frown and places them on his own lap. Mary gives Evan a glare but doesn't argue with him.

"Now, Nan, explain," he demands.

"Well I was talking to Kennedy here and she explained her situation. Now I want to know how you're going to keep our girl and my grandbaby safe," she explains and my chest expands. Is she putting on a show for Evan because a few minutes ago I wasn't sure she even liked me, now she's calling me her girl?

"We're dealing with it," he groans, and looks to me with a look I can't figure out. It's probably him silently telling me I should have kept it shut, but then if he knew what she asked me, he would likely understand. Not that I'd tell him. He's already argued with one family member over me, I'm not causing another argument. Believe it or not, I actually want Imogen to grow up with a loving family around her. It's something I never had. The family I grew up with after my parents died were nice enough. But the minute I hit sixteen I was on my own.

ELEVEN

EVAN

OUT OF ALL THE DAYS MY nan has to show up, it has to be the day I decide to make a move on Kennedy. I made an excuse to go get some shit from the store, which we did need, but I needed condoms more.

She's been slowly driving me insane over the past few days with her curvy, tight body, her tits, her hair, the way she speaks so softly and the way she mothers Imogen. Something about seeing her attend to Imogen turns me on. It makes me want to see her with a rounded stomach, bare feet, and cooking in our kitchen.

I've officially gone crazy.

It's the only logical explanation I can come up with for all these thoughts running through my mind.

I'd been prepared to jump her as soon as I walked through the door, not able to hold back another second. But then I got back to the house and it all went straight out of the window. A man had knocked on the door when I walked up. He was there for nan. But still, at first it nerved me wondering who he was and why he was there.

Then to top it off, my nan not only ruins my moment to seduce Kennedy, but ruins my sex life for good when she mentions her own. She's always been like this. The woman has no filter. I'd avoid her at all costs, but she's the kindest, most loving and loyal person you could ever know and I love her. She's always been there for us, especially Denny, since we were little. She could always see through everything going on at home and knew that they made Denny's life hell and, although she lived hours away, she still tried her hardest to make things better for both of us.

"So he won't hurt her? Because I'm telling you now, Evan Smith, if she gets hurt...again, it will kill me. My heart can't take it anymore. After Denny's assault I haven't been the same," Nan tells me with a sad face, and I officially feel like shit. I always expected my Nan to outlive us all.

"Nan, I promise, I got it handled. And have you had your heart checked out?" I ask gently, and Kennedy gives my thigh a squeeze. I turn giving her an encouraging smile before turning back to my Nan.

"Trust me; your nan has years left in her, Son. She has more stamina in her then what any woman did when I was your age," Peter brags, winking at me.

Fucking winked at me.

She's my nan, asshole.

I growl in anger, but Nan laughs it off and puts her hand on fucking Peter's thigh, giving it a squeeze. "Why don't you get the bags, darling, they're by the door," she tells him smiling.

He gets up like a good lap dog, grabbing a hundred bags from the hall.

"What the hell?" I ask, seeing baby brand names on most of the bags.

"Why don't you finish feeding Imogen while I show you what I got? She needs winding," Nan asks, smiling at Kennedy. Kennedy stands up and I follow, quickly grabbing her by the hips to sit her back down. I kick the foot muff next to the chair she's sitting on before walking over, quickly grabbing Immy.

"Hey, princess, you enjoyed meeting your, Nana?" I coo, smiling at her.

She doesn't make a noise, but that doesn't bother me. She's still so tiny and I know she's behind in her development. I don't care though; I know she'll succeed in the future. With hard work and good parents she'll do it. I'm sure of it.

"Now, I got this for Kennedy," Nan starts pulling out some ear plugs.

"Nan!" I yell, offended. "She's not going to ignore Immy when she cries."

"That's not why I got them. They're so she doesn't have to lose sleep listening to you snore," she snaps, but looks amused. I look to Kennedy for help. For her to tell my nan that I don't snore, but she just giggles harder. I send her a glare and turn back to nan. I can't help but wonder if I do. It's not like I'll know. But still, Kennedy and I had to share a bed the past two nights 'cause of how cold it was in the front room. The radiator broke, so only the bedroom ones work.

"And this is for you, grumpy. Hopefully they'll cheer you up," Nan winks then throws a box at my feet. I look horrified and wish to God I could hide them before Kennedy sees them. I know it's too late when she chokes on laughter.

"Glad someone finds it funny," I grumble staring down horrified at the box of condoms, but it only makes her laugh harder.

"Peter said to get you some lube. That young ones today love all the backdoor business," she states and I choke on my words. I choke that hard Kennedy has to take Immy off me to finish feeding her.

"Jesus, Nan. You couldn't have just bought me a watch?" I groan. She used to buy me them as a kid and even as a successful detective, who is badass, if I say so myself, she still got them me for birthdays and Christmases. And each one would have some stupid cartoon character on it or some wise saying on the face or on the back of the watch.

"Sorry. Denny has told me to tone it down, but I just want to be *in* with the in crowd. I don't want to be one of those snotty, knitting, sagging, buggy pushers that need help wiping their own asses and finding out what new is going on in the world by reading a boring newspaper."

She's fucking blunt I'll give her that. I want to laugh, but it will just give her more ammunition, like Kennedy is currently doing now by laughing. I give her a glare but she just blushes, looking down at her lap.

"Nan, one day you'll be in a home..." I begin, needing her to understand.

"Young boy, go wash your mouth out. If I go in a home you grandkids are moving in with me and your spouses, and your kids, and every fucker else I know. The only way you'll get me into one of them old bag homes is when my body is stone cold and six feet under, and even then it will be against my will."

"Seriously, just, just stop," I plead, feeling a headache forming.

I listen to her go on about everything she bought, explaining each outfit and toy to us. It's driving me mad, but Kennedy doesn't seem to mind. When she starts going on about getting Imogen christened, I know it's time to say goodbye.

If and when we decided to get Imogen christened, I want it to be mine and Kennedy's decision, not my nan forcing us to.

"It was so lovely to meet you, honey. I promise to get in touch with Denny and explain everything," she whispers to Kennedy, thinking I can't hear. I give her a growl and gently push her more out of the door.

When they're gone I shut the door behind us and lean back against it, taking in a deep breath. It feels like I've been holding my breath since the box of condoms came out.

The door knocks behind me and I look at Kennedy with wide eyes.

"Maybe if we pretend we're not here she'll go away," I whisper to Kennedy, wondering what would bring her back here.

Kennedy laughs and pushes me out of the way to open the door, but soon stops when she sees who is on the other side.

What the fuck?

Peeping around the door frame, my hands automatically go to Kennedy's waist. Lexi is standing there in the pouring rain. She looks sad, lost, and I can't help but not feel sorry for her. I feel like she pushed me away as a friend when she started dating. Ever since Kennedy moved in, Lexi has been coming round here more and more, asking me to fix something in her apartment. Even if I wasn't her landlord I'd still do it, I'm not a complete jerk, but enough is enough. How much more could break in her house?

"Oh, hey, Lexi."

"You didn't come," she states sadly, and I look to her confused when I hear a whispered 'fudge' coming from Kennedy. The fact she doesn't swear is so fucking hot, but the words she replaces them with are fucking hilarious. When she says 'ohmygosh' I have to fight back tears of laughter.

"Sorry, we had visitors. I was just getting around to telling him," Kennedy explains brightly, but I can hear the bite in her tone.

Is my girl jealous? I'm grinning inwardly just thinking about it.

"No problem," Lexi answers, and I look away from Kennedy to get the receiving end of a funny look she'd been giving Kennedy. It seems I've missed something over the past week that I shouldn't have.

"What did you need?" I ask, keeping my voice pleasant even when I want to shout at her to leave. We got Immy to sleep ten minutes before Nan and her bloke left, so we've got a couple of hours at the most before she wakes up. I don't want to have to spend that time fixing a bloody window latch. I want to spend it with my woman under me crying out my name.

"The, um, the sink is leaking. I can't get it to stop," she tells me smiling, but looks more like a cringe.

The shift in her mood surprises me and I quickly look down at my watch noticing it's still before five. They'll be open. "I've got a number for a local plumber. Give him a call and I'll foot the bill," I tell her, about to turn to grab the card from my wallet.

"I'm sure it's nothing," she rushes out. "Can you just take five minutes to look at it?" she asks, her tone pleading. I look down to Kennedy and she just looks up at me shrugging.

She's no freaking help.

I groan.

"Okay, but if it needs work I'll have to call him myself," I tell her. I move away from the door leaving Kennedy standing there while I grab my coat and wallet, just in case I need to give them a call. Kennedy is still standing by the door when I return and I lean down giving her a kiss on the forehead before ducking under the rain and rushing around to Lexi's place.

We rush into the apartment, the rain already drenching my skin. Not wanting to mess around with pleasantries I walk straight over to the kitchen sink, noticing there isn't a leak.

"Lexi, there's nothing wrong with the sink," I tell her, turning around. "What the hell?" I shout, turning back around and covering my eyes. Lexi is standing in the closed doorway in nothing but her knickers. Yes, I noticed, sue me, I'm a bloke.

What I didn't expect was this kind of boldness coming from her.

Especially her.

This is nothing like the Lexi I've come to know. If this had happened a few months ago I'd probably be hard as a rock right now and jumping at the chance, but it's not. Now I have Kennedy in my life and I'm not foolish enough to jeopardise that. She's special, but, more importantly she's someone I can see myself having a future with. It's just a bonus she's the mother of my daughter, whether she gave birth to her or not.

"Don't you still want me? I made a mistake, Evan. I want you," she says seductively, her voice sounding closer. I move around the counter towards the front door. I'm surprised I made it there safely with my hands still covering my eyes.

"Lexi, you don't want me. You made your choice crystal clear. I have Kennedy and Imogen now."

"Then why can't you look at me? You want me, admit it," she cries loudly and I turn around feeling pissed.

How dare she?

Looking straight into her eyes I switch on my interrogation mask, wanting her to know I'm deadly fucking serious. "Lexi, I'm not looking at you due to respect for you and for Kennedy, who by the way is next door with my daughter. I don't know why the sudden change, but you don't want me, and if I'm honest, I never really wanted you. I wanted what my sister had. I have that now. With Kennedy. You need to stop whatever this is and move on," I wave at her.

I sigh, feeling disgusted for staying as long as I have. Turning, I leave, slamming the door behind me and blocking out Lexi's sobs. There's one thing I have a huge weakness for and that's crying women. I hate seeing them upset and hurt. I always want to try and fix it.

Walking back into mine, I give one look to Kennedy who is curled up on the couch and sag with relief. This is where I want to be, where I need to be and with Kennedy, I know I'll be here until she tells me to leave.

"Hey, what's wrong?" she asks voicing her concern when I sit down after taking my wet coat off.

"Lexi," I groan, wondering how to tell her.

"I'm taking it she told you she wanted you?" she says, shocking me.

"What? Huh?"

"Oh come on, the woman has been pining over you ever since I arrived. She wants me gone, that much is obvious. So, how did it go?" she asks, her voice and facial expression dropping towards the end.

"She got naked," I blurt out.

Kennedy shoots up from the couch and I follow.

Shit.

When her eyes start to water I feel like shit and begin to wish I never said anything. Like I said, I hate women crying, but seeing Kennedy cry is tearing my heart out.

"Please don't cry. I don't want her, I want you. I promise I didn't even look at her. I got out of there as soon as I could," I tell her quickly, needing her to know how much she means to me.

"So you didn't... Nothing happened?" she croaks out.

"No. Never! I promise. I'd never do that to you, babe."

"Fudging hell! We've been giving this a go between us for not even a week and I've already gone all territorial on your bum," she groans making me chuckle. If only she knew how unbelievably hot it is watching her riled up over it all.

"I think it's brilliant, and hot, and sexy," I whisper to her, bending my head down to give her a kiss. She reaches up on her toes, meeting me for the kiss.

The minute my lips touch hers I'm lost. Lost in her and lost in the kiss. Damn this woman. She can bring me to my knees with one simple touch.

My hands reach for her jumper and I slowly pull away when I start to lift it up her body. She's shaking and I can see goosebumps breaking out all over her skin and chest.

The second her jumper hits the floor my mouth reaches for hers again in a heated, passionate kiss.

I'm about to grab my own t-shirt that is damp from walking across to Lexi's and back when Imogen starts crying. I groan into the kiss hoping she'll stop, but when her cries get louder I push away from Kennedy feeling frustrated as fuck. I've never wanted to be inside a woman as much as I do her.

"I think my daughter is cock blocking me," I moan.

Kennedy laughs, her cheeks flushed and her lips swollen. She reaches down for her jumper and I try to stop her from putting it back on.

"I'll go settle her down."

She giggles looking down at my crotch. "Um. I think *you* should settle down first." With that she walks down the hall towards Imogen's nursery, still chuckling.

Little minx.

TWELVE

KENNEDY

WAITING TABLES WAS THE LAST thing I wanted to do when I woke up this morning. Especially since I could be at home with Imogen and Evan, but my time off, including Evan's, had come to an end.

Spending so much time together over the past week has brought all three of us closer together. I know Imogen is too young to realise anything has changed but even she has grown attached to everything that is Evan.

Already Evan has picked up on what Imogen's tells are, what her likes and dislikes are and how to settle her down. They've bonded in the way I had hoped they would. I shouldn't have been worried.

Evan and I have also gotten to know each other on a deeper level. We talked about our pasts, our families and growing up. We talked about our likes and dislikes and have grown closer over the week. It feels like we've known each other a lot longer and he even admitted I knew more about him than any of his friends.

Thinking of Evan, his body and his personality, reminds me just how lucky I am to have him in my life. Never in a million years would I have thought a man like him would ever look twice at me. But for some reason he has. I'll never understand it and, if I'm honest, I don't quite believe it, but for some reason I know I'll live with it. He's everything a girl could wish for in a bloke.

Evan is the first man I've ever lived with intimately and it's taken a lot to get used to it. Not in the way you may think. I guess I'm used to my privacy, my own space. When I got an upset stomach from the dinner I thought he cooked, but instead he ordered in, I had been in so much pain that I knew I needed to go to the toilet. I'd been completely mortified. I don't know about anyone else but that's the worst part of a relationship for me. But it shows how comfortable I am with him because I excused myself and did my business. Mind you, I've only been in that situation once before and it was when I was round my ex-boyfriend's house. I had caught a stomach bug and desperately needed the toilet. Even though we had been dating for over a year I still didn't feel comfortable enough to go to the toilet around him, so I ended up leaving in a hurry to get home.

I guess what I'm trying to say is, I don't feel unwelcome, I feel comfortable. I know he wouldn't act immature and make an issue or a scene just to embarrass me. It's not like women don't go to the toilet, it's just not very lady-like or seductive. The other part is that I don't mind going through stuff when I clean, or making myself at home. In fact, we seem to pretty much work together like we've been doing it for twenty years.

The only things I've still not gotten used to is having to put the toilet seat back down when he's left it up. It's not good going to the toilet early hours of the morning, half asleep, only to fall into it because he forgot to put the toilet seat down.

The other major one is his idea of cleaning. He shoves things in cupboards without a care in the world, he never polishes and I'm pretty sure he didn't know he had a hoover. Biggest pet peeve though is spending hours ironing his clothes, for him to just throw them into his wardrobe, not bothering to hang them up or fold them away in his drawers? We had words about this one. It went pretty much how I thought it would. He kissed me making me forget what we were talking about in the first place.

But the one thing I've found the hardest to get used to is sharing a bed. Even though we've done nothing sexually, the tension is there and it's suffocating. I've been finding it hard to sleep because of it, but there are also other reasons. The main reason is because I like to sleep in the middle. I'm used to sleeping like a starfish, not caring if my mouth is hanging open or if I'm drooling in my sleep.

Now, I have to give up the middle of the bed and I'm constantly trying to cover my mouth with the blanket just in case I accidentally move it away and have my mouth hanging open like a goon.

Hey, it happens.

"Order up," Howard shouts from the kitchen, snapping me from my thoughts. I rush through with the drinks I was just filling to a table before moving over to the hotplate stand. I rip off the table number and groan when I find the food's for table four. Three men walked in over an hour ago now and have only just ordered food. When they first arrived something in the air shifted. I'm not usually one to judge but the three men looked like serious trouble. And you know what they say; if it smells like trouble, looks like trouble, then it most likely is trouble, and these three men were definitely trouble. It's like they're waiting for something or someone and it unnerves me, especially when I've found the biggest one of the three staring at me more than once. Each and every time I've felt his eyes on me a cold shiver has ran down my back.

If they're here to deal drugs to someone then they'll be extremely disappointed. Mark, co-owner of Molly's, used to be a copper. He still takes the term 'serve and protect' seriously, even if he is retired. He won't stand for... you know...mess like that going on in his cafe.

Thankfully I get off in a couple of hours and won't have to worry about them. I've been dead on my feet since nine this morning. It's now five in the evening and I'll have to pick up Imogen from Melanie's soon. With the weather being so bad her day care had called me this morning telling me they were closed for the day. Apparently most of their staff travel from a small village half an hour away and it's all flooded. They apologised profusely and explained it was too short notice to get any substitute teachers in to cover for them.

"Can I get you anything else?" I ask as I drop the three plates down, trying not to curse. I usually only carry two plates at a time, but because I didn't want to hang around them any longer than necessary, I placed one of the plates along my arm, and the hot plate has burnt my pale skin, leaving an angry red mark.

"Yeah, how about your number?" the biggest of the three laughs slapping my ass. I squeal, jumping away and sending him a glare, even though my heart is thumping in my chest.

"If that's all, I'll leave you to your food," I snap, not caring if I get into trouble. I don't deserve to be harassed. *Customers are always right* my butt.

"Hey, not so fast. How about you join us?" the smaller of the three winks making me cringe.

"No, thank you," I tell him sternly before walking off. On my way back to the counter I drop off some extra napkins to a family when I hear the three men saying something crude about my behind.

"Yo, Kennedy, you got a call," a loud booming voice shouts across the restaurant. I jump where I'm standing before looking over to find Molly waving the phone in the air. I walk over taking the phone off him, giving him a smug smile.

He's always complaining no one ever calls him. Any time the phone rings it's either for bookings or for one of the other staff working. Granted, I've only ever been called a few times due to emergencies, one of them being my sister being found dead. So having a call has the hairs on the back of my neck stand up. Nothing good ever comes from having a phone call at work.

"Hello?"

"Kennedy?"

"Melanie? Is that you? Is Imogen okay?" I ask panicked, a horrible feeling sinking in the pit of my stomach.

"Yeah, she's fine. I went over to your place to get her lullaby pen to settle her down a little. She's been grumpy all afternoon. I think it's her teeth again. But when I went over," she says pausing, as if she's debating whether to tell me or not.

"What is it, just tell me?" I tell her needing her to just hit me with it. Whatever it is I can handle it. Nothing could be worse than what happened to me last week or the threat on Imogen's life.

"Your place is completely trashed. I'm sorry, honey."

I gasp down the phone, tears filling my eyes. Not wanting to cry until I know how much damage there is I straighten up, not wanting to break down at work. But no matter how much I try the lump in my throat grows. All I can think about is how much money it will cost. No matter how many hours at work I do, I'll never be able to replace everything in my flat. I'm already lucky to have what I do in there. It's not much, but I bought it all with hard earned money. Now it looks like I'll have to do it all over again. I can't expect Evan to support me and Imogen forever. The guy won't even let me buy food for honey's sake. If he finds out about this I know he'll demand to replace it all and I can't...no, won't have that. I don't need a man to look after me. Okay, that's a half lie. I may not need a man to look after me, but I do want Evan to care for me.

"Let me talk to Mo. I'm going to try get over there as soon as possible. It's pretty busy in here today." It's not a lie either. My feet are killing me from being on them all day and after having the week off doing hardly anything, they're not used to being on the go so much. I guess a week off really does do wonders to a person.

"Do you want me to call the police?"

I think it over for a second before answering her. Honestly, I couldn't care less about the flat. I know they'll never catch anyone or pay for it to be replaced, but still, it was home. "Let me come assess the damage, otherwise I'll never get in there if the police are involved. I'll call Evan on the way over, see what he says."

"Okay, sweetie. I'll just see if her pen is usable before I lock up behind me. Be careful on the roads, the weather's getting worse out there. Earlier I thought the window was going to smash it was raining that hard."

"I will," I laugh. "See you in a bit," I tell her. I wait for her to say goodbye but the line goes dead. Thinking it must have been cut off by the weather I make my way over to the kitchen to Mo.

"Mo?" I call when I reach the kitchen. He gives me a look that says *I know what you want*. I give him a wide smile, knowing he can't resist or say no to me.

Mo is a large loveable man and without him I would never have been able to raise Imogen on my own, especially without having to depend on government support. He made sure to be fair when it came to my hours and always, always, lets me take my own tips home. The rest of the staff put theirs in a pot and at the end of each month it's shared out equally. I tried to refuse, not wanting to be singled out, but because all the other staff members are either old or have no family, they said it was only fair. They even give me a percentage of their tips if my own tips are low at the end of each week.

"Go. Do whatever you gotta do, but girl, you owe me hours. God, you're a pain in my ass," he scolds holding up a spatula.

"Okay, and you love me really," I giggle.

"Get gone," he shouts, his lips twitching.

Giggling, I move into the staffroom to grab my keys and coat out of my locker. For once, I'm thankful I have my piece of poop car. Evan had taken me to get it this morning when he came with me to drop Imogen off with Melanie.

Remembering this morning when we dropped Imogen off brings me back to Evan leaving for work. He found it hard to leave Imogen, it was cute. A few times he even contemplated calling in and just staying at home with Imogen. He even tried to bribe me to call in sick, but I knew I couldn't afford any more time off. I didn't say that to him, though. I don't want him to know how hard I struggle. He probably has an idea already, but I don't want to wave the poor flag in front of his face. I keep forgetting he has seen this mess I live in. No one with money would choose to live there.

I wave goodbye as I leave, walking back through the kitchen. I'd parked my car out the back today, not wanting to have to park miles down the road like I normally have to.

Running through the rain over to where my car is parked I end up soaked. The rain is coming down heavier and I start to feel worried about driving in it. My flat is only fifteen minutes tops drive away, but in this weather, I'd be lucky if I get there in thirty. My car isn't the best to handle and the wind isn't exactly on my side tonight either.

Shivering, I start up the car, turning the heater on full blast. When cold wind blows through the air vents I shiver uncontrollably. I really should start saving for a new car. I sit for a few more minutes waiting for the heater to warm up.

When it's warm enough I reverse out of my spot with ease. The roads are slick as I pull out onto the main road. There aren't many cars around which eases my worry about driving. I'm not at all surprised that no one is out driving in this. You'd have to be insane. Like me.

Grabbing my phone from my pocket I dial Evan's number to update him on what's going on. Evan seems like a man who would get pissed if I didn't tell him about something as important as this. The phone rings and rings and I let it ring to voicemail before ending the call. Deciding to leave it for a few more minutes, I put on the radio to distract me from the disaster I'm about to walk into.

My only concern about turning up at my flat is that I'll find out it has something to do with Damon. Maybe he knows I'm not living there at the moment and smashed it up. In reality it could just be some punk kids who live in the same block of flats as me that have noticed I'm not there and have decided to see what they could rob. I'm praying for the latter, but no matter how much I tell myself that it's just a bunch of kids, a sinking feeling in the pit of my stomach is telling me it's Damon, and I need to be prepared for what's to come.

Dialling Evan again, I wait for him to answer, but it rings straight to voicemail. This time I decide to leave a message hoping he'll listen to it before I arrive at the flat.

"Hey, Evan, it's me, Kennedy," I start, groaning at how dorky I sound. I fudging hate leaving voicemails. My voice never sounds like me and I hate it. I sound more like a little girl sucking on helium. "I'm heading over to my place. Melanie called and said there was a break-in and the place is trashed. Call me back when you get this."

As soon as I've ended the call my phone begins to vibrate in my hand causing me to jump. I don't usually talk on my phone when I'm driving, but when I notice Melanie's name is flashing on the screen, I answer.

"Oh, Kennedy! Kennedy," she sobs and my heart stops. "I'm so sorry."

"Melanie! Melanie! Calm down," I shout, the signal weakening as I drive through a small tunnel.

"She's gone," she cries down the phone, her voice breaking up.

"Who's gone?" I ask, fear evident in my voice. In my heart I know who she's going to say, my heart is already breaking, but my head is refusing to believe that this is happening.

"Imogen," she sobs, her cries echoing down the line. And just like that my whole world stops. Staring ahead at nothing is all I do for a beat; I don't even take a breath. My mind is screaming 'no it's not true, this can't be happening'. She's a baby. With shaky hands I end the call without a word, not even to comfort Melanie or ask any questions. Nothing feels real. Not the rain pounding on the windscreen, or the sound of my tyres splashing through the rain. Even the radio that is still crackling is like white noise.

Another driver blasts his horn at me, the sound snapping me out of my haze. The car has steered to the right, so I quickly straighten it up before taking in a deep breath.

"Imogen," I cry, a sob ripping free, tears flowing freely down my face. I wipe them away furiously. Now isn't the time to get upset. She needs me.

My heart cracks a little bit more and I know I can't do this on my own. I need, Evan. He's the only person who can help me, who can save Imogen.

Oh, God. He just got her, and now someone's taken her away from him because of me. Because of my fudging sister. I should have known something was going to happen. I shouldn't have gone to work like Evan asked me to. This is all my fault.

Slamming my hands on the steering wheel I cry out in frustration and pain.

Pressing down on the accelerator the car slowly begins to speed up, the engine groaning in protest. My mind screams at me to slow down, to think clearly, but I need to get to Imogen. I need to do something. She can't be gone. She's mine. She's my baby. It's not true. It can't be.

Grabbing my phone again I redial Evan, needing him more than I've ever needed anyone in my whole darn life. If anyone knows what to do it's him. Just dialling his number relaxes me somewhat. I know he'll do everything in his power to get Imogen back. I just hope he doesn't hate me when he finds out she's gone.

"Goddamn it, Evan," I scream, listening to his voicemail once again. "Evan," I sob, hoping he can hear me since my phone keeps beeping, alerting me that I'm losing signal. I feel like I'm about to lose my mind. My hands are shaking wildly as I drive as fast as I can through the streets. "It's Imogen, she's gone. Melanie said she's gone-" The phone slips from my fingers because of them shaking so badly, so I don't get to finish what I was going to say. It falls against my thigh before smashing against something near the handbrake, a choking noise escaping my throat at the sound.

Scared, desperate, and needing him, I try to grab for my phone, not ready to give up. That's when everything happens. That's when my whole life flashes before my very eyes and I scream out in a panic.

The car swerves to the left hand side of the road and in a panic to try and control the wheel, I accidentally press my foot down harder on the accelerator. It all happens so fast and before I have time to react I feel the colossal impact. The sound of metal crunching, glass smashing and the sound of my own screams fill the car. Cuts from the shards of glass cut into my face and arms. In a panic I spot blood dripping onto my lap. It causes another mild panic attack. Slowly, with shaking hands, I lift them to my head, wincing when I feel a gash there.

Suddenly everything around me comes to a standstill, the deafening noise of horns blaring and the people's screams stop. The only sound I can hear is the rain hitting the roof of the car.

Looking around me in a daze I try to think about what happened. Everything seems to be moving slowly. My eyes move to the windshield, squinting when bright lights shine through blinding me.

It takes me a couple of seconds to realise what is going to happen, my eyes widen for a fraction of a second and I brace for impact, covering my head with my arms. I barely have time to reach up before the sickening crunch of metal hits my ears. My whole body is jerked to the right side of the car, my head smashing against the door. Images of Imogen and our life flicker through my mind like a slideshow just before everything turns black, silencing all the chaos that is going on around me.

THIRTEEN

EVAN

"YOU REALLY NEED TO GET YOUR head out of your ass," Harris grumbles to the side of me. We're currently sneaking under some thorn bushes and it's fucking freezing as hell. Not to mention it's pouring down with rain and we're both soaking wet. He tells me to get my head out of my ass but what I really fucking need are my girls, a warm dinner inside me and a chilled beer. But at this moment in time a cup of hot chocolate wouldn't go a miss.

"Fuck off," I snap, my teeth clattering together. Fuck it's cold.

"Come on, fucker. Show your face," Harris mumbles as he slides his body towards the farthest end of the bush. Once he's in position he pulls the camera from behind his back. I follow suit grabbing mine. We're hoping this new position will finally be able to give us a clear view of who the dealer is.

A dad has hired us to get some evidence against the person who murdered his thirteen year old daughter who died from an overdose. He turned up at our offices giving us all the information he could get on who the dealer is, telling us the police needed more evidence before making an arrest. Most of the information he had was just hearsay, but it did help point us in the right direction. After all, we could do things that the police couldn't.

We've got a team of officers on standby for when we get the money photo, but until then we're freezing our asses off in the freezing cold. If we don't get this money photo then we're basically screwed.

"So, when do I get to meet this new piece of ass?" Harris grins and I turn giving him a glare.

"Never, you fucking wanker. And she's not a piece of ass, you dickhead," I whisper yell across to him. Gritting my teeth, I warn him. "And if you call her that again, I'll punch your teeth down your throat."

He chuckles, not bothered by my outburst. "Oh yeah? So no chance of tag teaming?" he asks and I lose my shit. I'm about to put him on his ass, well up on his feet so I can put him on his ass, when he gives me the signal, his features turning serious. Looking through the lens of my camera I suck in an audible breath before snapping picture after picture, wanting to make sure I get the whole encounter.

"Fuck me," I breathe.

"Holy fuck!" Harris curses. Wasting no time he grabs his phone and calls it in. Just as he puts the phone down my own phone vibrates in my pocket, reminding me that I have a voicemail that's been left unanswered. It got left around half an hour ago. I'd been too busy with the job to even look at the screen to see who it was, so I'm hoping it's nothing important.

"Got him," I grin as I snap another photo of the bloke the dad is accusing of selling bad drugs to his daughter.

I'm about to turn around to call out to Harris but the little fucker has snuck up on me instead. We end up smacking our knuckles together and grinning like two fucking idiots. It's jobs like this one that helps me remember why I do what I do for a living. I fucking hate scumbags like this deadbeat who sell drugs to kids like it's a respectable living. Not caring about the consequences of his actions or if the buyer is underage. They're the lowest of the low.

"Let's go," he grins.

I grin in return, thankful to be able to get home to my girls. Thinking of my girls I grab my phone out of my pocket.

I've never had to consider anyone when I'm working. Whenever I've gotten phone calls or messages during a job I've always presumed it was my boss or someone else on the case. With the girls moving in it should have crossed my mind that it could be Kennedy that called me.

Looking down at my phone it blinks with two missed calls from Kennedy and one from an unknown number.

Fuck's sake. First time back at work, she calls me and I don't fucking answer. She could need something and I wasn't there for her. What a way to show her I'm reliable.

Walking to the car I click on the voicemail that Kennedy left me, smiling when I hear her voice. My smile soon falls when I hear what she says.

"Hey, Evan, it's me, Kennedy," she says pausing and I have to chuckle at how awkward she sounds. "I'm heading over to my place. Melanie called and said there was a break-in and that the place is trashed. Call me back when you get this."

"Fuck!" I hiss. She better not have gone there. It could be a trap or worse, it could be a warning. She doesn't need to see the mess her place is in, or see any surprises that could be left. I feel like a bigger wanker now for not answering.

"What?" Harris asks, looking at me curiously.

"We need to go. Kennedy's place got broken into and she's heading over there," I tell him quickly. I'm torn over listening to the next voicemail or calling her back and telling her to wait for me to get there. But then she could have left another voicemail telling me that everything's okay.

The sick feeling that's been churning in my gut all fucking morning comes back, so I hit number one on my phone to listen to the next message.

"Evan," Kennedy cries frantically down the phone and my heart fucking stops. I'm running over to the car as fast as my legs will take me when her next words have me crumbling to the floor. "It's Imogen, she's gone. Melanie said she's gone," is all she manages to say before horns blare, deafening me, glass smashes and tyres are screeching through the phone.

Fuck no! Please, fuck no!

"Kennedy! Fuck, Kennedy," I shout, not caring that she can't hear me. The voicemail cuts off leaving me with nothing more.

Getting up off the floor I race to the car, thankful Harris hadn't seen my fall and had carried on to the car. The car is running when I jump into the passenger seat. It's not until I'm sitting in the front that I realise I have no clue what the fuck I'm doing.

Kennedy has been in an accident, if it was an accident, and Immy has gone missing. I wish like fuck I could rip myself in half. Then one could run to Immy and one could get to Kennedy.

"We need to go to the hospital," I tell him trying to keep my calm. I feel his eyes on me so I turn to see his look of concern. He must see I'm deadly fucking serious because I'm jerked back into my seat as he speeds off.

I'm glad I programmed Melanie's number into my phone this morning. I had wanted to make sure she had a way of contacting either me or Kennedy if anything happened. Really, I just wanted to check in on Immy throughout the day, but I haven't been able to get five minutes. I wish I had made that five minutes happen, at least then I might have been able to do something.

I'm just hoping Kennedy's mistaken and Immy isn't gone, but in my gut I know it's true. I can somehow feel it. It's the same feeling I've had since I woke up this morning. I thought it was about the job I knew we would be on today. If I knew my girls would be at risk I wouldn't have let any of us leave the house.

"Oh my God, Evan. Kennedy hasn't arrived yet and I'm beginning to worry. She should be here. The police keep asking me all these questions and I don't know anything," Melanie cries, her voice hoarse. "I'm so sorry. So fucking sorry."

"Miss, we need you to answer some more questions," someone in the background asks stiffly.

Prick.

He could be more sympathetic. A child has been taken and it's clear Melanie is hysterical and needs calming down. Making her answer the same questions over and over will just cause her anxiety to increase.

"No, I don't. I need to answer the father's questions. He needs to get his little girl back," she snaps sniffling. I find myself respecting her in that moment, but hearing her say 'father' and 'his little girl' causes my chest to tighten.

I'm trying my hardest to keep my cool, I really am, but fuck, she's my little girl and I've just got her. She's out there with complete strangers and they're doing fuck knows what. This morning she hadn't been in the best of moods because her teeth were bothering her. The fact she's in that mood and with people who don't know anything about her spikes my anger.

"Melanie, I need you to calm down for me. What happened?"

"I went over to Kennedy's to get Imogen's music pen, hoping it would settle her down, and when I got there Kennedy's place was a complete mess. I quickly called her and she told me she was on her way. I was going to see if the pen was still in working order. I swear; I was gone two minutes tops. When I got back home

Imogen was gone. Just gone."

My heart sinks and my hands clench into tight fists. I want to kill someone. I know who did this but I need to have some sort of proof. I begin punching the fuck out of the dashboard, not able to hold in my anger any longer. The pain in my fist does nothing to release the aggression inside me, it only fuels it more.

"Evan! Fuck! Calm the fuck down," Harris shouts across the car, his arm smacking me in the chest and holding me back. I breathe heavily, my chest heaving. Melanie says something down the phone that I don't quite hear, but it's enough to bring me back to the present.

"Okay. Okay," I say shaking my head and running my hands through my wet hair. "Did you see anyone unusual? Someone you've not seen before that seemed curious with you or Kennedy's place?" I ask, my academy training finally sinking in.

"I... No...Oh, no wait. There was a guy yesterday knocking on her door for a good twenty minutes. He had a scar down his face. I also noticed him this morning outside just before you guys turned up. I didn't think anything of it. God, this is all my fault. That poor little baby. What have I done?" she sobs and my heart breaks knowing all too well who she is on about.

"This isn't your fault, Melanie. You're lucky you weren't there to get in the way. He would have killed you," I tell her honestly, thinking back to his rap sheet. He's brutal. We've never been able to get any charges to stick though. When I went to the station he was smug. He knew we couldn't charge him because of his tight alibi.

"You know him? You can get her back? Where is Kennedy?" she asks somewhat calmer.

"I think she's been in an accident," I tell her, pinching the bridge of my nose. I'm torn about what to do. Find my girl or go to my woman. As soon as I've checked to make sure she was indeed in an accident and is okay, I'll go home and find everything I can about this son of a bitch. He's going to wish he never messed with Kennedy or Imogen when I'm through with him.

"Oh, my God. Where? I'll be there..."

"Miss, you can't leave," an officer tells her.

"Melanie, I have to go. We're just pulling up at the hospital. Stay where you are and I'll call you when I find anything out," I tell her.

"Okay, okay," she rushes out and I end the call. Harris turns to me with worried eyes, but I don't wait around for his questioning. The car is still moving when I remove my belt and jump out of the car. Harris honks his horn and shouts obscenities out of the window but I ignore him, jumping over the bonnet and rushing through the emergency doors.

"Hi, I'm detective Smith. My fiancé, Kennedy, I think she was in an accident around half an hour ago. Can you tell me if she's here?" I ask the receptionist frantically. She looks at me with a sad smile and I want to snap at her to hurry the fuck up, I haven't got time to waste.

"What's her name, sir?"

"Kennedy. Kennedy Wright."

She types quickly onto the computer but then a man with a white lab coat walks around the desk looking at me. My eyes meet his and I know in my gut it's bad.

"Are you a relation to, Miss. Wright?" he asks, putting his hand up to the receptionist to stop her search.

"Yes, I'm her fiancé." I lie easily and I do it because I know it won't be long until she does have a ring around her finger and is taking my last name.

"Your fiancé was brought in not long ago with severe head trauma and multiple injuries," he starts and I follow him as he takes me down a long corridor. Out of nowhere Harris is standing next me and, if I'm honest, I'm thankful that he's here. There's only so much I can take before I explode again.

"Is she okay?" I ask when he stops short suddenly.

"It's too early to tell. She has a broken leg, fractured ribs and a lot of cuts and bruises. At this time we're concentrating on her head injury. Her broken leg won't be put in a cast until the swelling reduces considerably. We've managed to clean up all her scrapes and wrap up her ribs. Her head is another matter right now. We're waiting for the CT scan room to open up so we can send her down. Once we have the results we'll be able to tell you more about her diagnosis."

I groan into my hands suddenly feeling sick. She needs to be okay. She has to be. She has Imogen to look after. I need her. Imogen needs her.

Fuck! Imogen.

The doctor opens the door to a private room and gestures me inside. I wish he had prepared me more for what I'm about to see because as soon as I see her small, fragile frame lying down on the bed, broken and bruised, I collapse to the floor on my knees. I've seen crimes that will make people sick to the stomach, been called out to scenes that have been horrific, but nothing could have prepared me to see someone I've come to love lying helplessly in bed, not knowing if she's going to be okay.

I've never seen her look so vulnerable. Not even the time I turned up at her flat and she had been attacked.

Her head is swollen, cuts and bruises swelling her face further. She's unrecognisable. The pounding in my chest tightens and I feel like I'm suffocating.

"Is she in pain?" I whisper, my heart hurting for her.

"We've made her comfortable," the doctor answers from the end of Kennedy's bed.

Not caring who sees me, I sob into my hands, my head cast down feeling defeated. I let this happen. I should have been there for her. I should have let her drive my piece of shit car knowing I only needed to get to our building block. I should have done a lot of this differently this morning but my biggest regret was not telling Kennedy that I love her. In only a week, I've given the woman my heart and my soul. I'd die for her.

Why the fuck is this happening? She's a good person. She deserves a long, full, happy life. She doesn't deserve the life she's been given, not at all. It's unfair.

Standing up I walk to the edge of the bed, my anger simmering to boiling point when I see her close up. Taking her delicate hand in mine I silently promise her to make all this right. Pulling away, my hands clench into fists and my jaw locks.

"Mate, you need to keep it together for a little while longer," Harris demands, snapping me out of my thoughts.

Wiping the tears from my cheeks, I look up at him knowing that he's right. There's no point in me standing around feeling angry and waiting for the doctors to tell me something when I have my little girl to find. And I know when Kennedy wakes up to find Imogen still missing, with me at her bed side, she will hate me forever. I can't have that.

"Doc, I need you to do me a favour. I know you're busy but our daughter, she's been kidnapped. It's how Kennedy got into an accident. I need to go find our little girl, but I don't like leaving her alone. Can you call me on this number if there are any changes, please?" I ask handing him my card. "Any at all, no matter how small."

He walks over towards me with a serious expression. Patting me on the shoulders he answers, "Of course. I have a few other patients that I need to see, but I will keep you updated."

"Thank you." I whisper, feeling gratitude.

Walking back over to Kennedy my heart starts to beat frantically at seeing her. Her face is pale, bruises and cuts marking her face. I bend down, my lips to her ear before whispering, "I'll find her, I promise. Just make sure you fight and be awake when we get back. I love you, Kennedy." I lift my head, giving her a soft kiss on the lips before leaving. Harris falls in step behind me without question. He hasn't asked any questions at all. He's blindly followed me around just looking out for me and waiting for my word. I'm guessing he's caught on to what's going on, though, and that's why he hasn't asked questions.

"What's the plan?" he asks once we're in the car, asking the first question since I listened to Kennedy's voicemail.

"No plan. I find him and I make him pay."

From the look on Harris' face he's not so down with the idea. His brain is practically running wild on how to stop me from doing stupid. Whatever he's thinking it won't work. I'm determined to find that fucker and make him pay.

Back at the bungalow I waste no time in rushing through the door, not shutting it behind me. Harris is on the phone barking orders at people. We had put a self-employed contractor on Damon, wanting to catch him in the act when he next did something, but for some reason the bloke decided to take the day off. Today of all fucking days.

I don't care who the fuck is out on a job. I want everyone I know on this one. I need to get my girl home. Getting her back home to her mother, back to me is my main priority.

Papers are scattered all over the floor in the front and for once I'm glad I won the argument with Kennedy over keeping them here. Not having the room in my office I had to keep them in the front room behind the chair. When she found out what they all were she wanted them out of the house. I couldn't blame her. If she knew half the shit that was written in these files she'd be sick to her stomach. I'm also willing to bet that the innocent light that constantly shines in her eyes each day will slowly disappear. She's pure, innocent, and doesn't deserve to be faced with the shit that's in these boxes. The pictures in the files aren't much better. Most of it is about the case involving her sister, but once I found out who had hurt

Kennedy, I also had everything that the police had on Damon White copied and sent over. One of the perks of still having mates on the inside.

"Fuck's sake," I shout feeling frustrated. Time is ticking away and the longer it takes me to find him, to find Imogen, is more time Imogen has to spend away from her mom and dad.

"Hey, Evan. Do you have a minute?" Lexi's voice asks sweetly.

"Fuck off, Lexi. I don't have time for your shit," I yell, throwing a file up the wall near to where she's standing. "Fuck!"

"What's wrong?" she asks not giving up.

"Lexi, seriously, my woman is in the hospital and my girl has been kidnapped by some fucking psychopath. I really don't have time for your shit right now," I shout, looking at her. I watch her flinch, her body tightening like I'd just struck her. I've never yelled at a woman like I just did her and I feel kind of shitty for it, or I would if I wasn't so fucking worried about Kennedy and Imogen.

Fuck's sake. She's all alone in that hospital with no family sitting by her side or to show their support. My daughter is out there, god knows where, and I dread to think of what situation she's in.

"Oh, Evan. What's happened? Who's with Kennedy?" she asks, only concern lacing her voice.

"No one," I whisper and slump down on the floor.

There is nothing in these files that tell me anything I don't already know.

He moved in with his dad and stepmom when he turned fourteen because of his junky mother. They are the only living relatives that he has. The police and co-workers of mine have already checked his usual hangout joints and have people asking around. But nothing has come up. There's no romantic relationship or regular hook-ups and over the last week of our contractor following him we know he doesn't have a patterned routine.

"I'll go to the hospital and sit with her. I'll tell them I'm her sister," Lexi says, but I ignore her when I hear her start talking to Harris. Something in this file has to help me find where the fuck he took my daughter. He has to have another place to go, somewhere he doesn't visit on a regular basis or hasn't been on the police radar.

Harris tells Lexi that it's a good idea but I have no idea what they're talking about. But then a name stands out in a file. The biological mother. Then it hits me. We've been hitting up his dad and step-mom's house when we should have been looking into his mother and her background. From what it says, she had no visitation rights to Damon, but when he turned eighteen he found her and they formed a relationship. Speculation in the file says she's the reason he got into selling drugs to begin with. His mom's poison is heroin, which is what the police think Damon sells, amongst other shit. He's known for other crimes too, anything to get his hands on money.

"Fuck!" I yell out, getting up off the floor. Aaron walks in at that moment looking around at the papers thrown across the room.

"You got anything?" he asks looking worried for me. Most likely for my sanity. I feel like I'm losing it, but then, if I lose the two most important people in my life, my sanity will be the least of his worries.

"Yeah. Were all these up-to-date when you had them copied and sent over?" I ask, pointing towards the mess.

"Yeah, why?"

"I think I know where he's taken her. Harris, you coming with me?" I shout before turning back around to Aaron, wondering for the first time who told him to come here. Last we heard he was getting the picture of Damon sent out to the local police stations. "How come you're here? Not that I mind, I could use all the help I can get."

"I'm picking up Lexi to take her to the hospital," he tells me, looking to his right where Lexi has thrown a bag of stuff together. Why the fuck is she packing her stuff? My anger rises again but then I notice that she's packed some of Imogen's belongings too. I look up to her confused, wondering what the hell she's up to. She must have sensed my stare because she stops what she's doing and turns to me.

"You're going to find her. You're going to get her back and when you do, she will need the comfort of her own things. I've got some things for Kennedy too. I know I've been a shitty friend and I've made things awkward between us. I came over to say I'm sorry. But then this happened, and I... I just want to be here for you all."

I give her a small smile, thankful that she's here and thought of all this. Kennedy has no one, just like Lexi. All her family either disowned her or passed away. Her ex wasn't the best of people, and her family weren't the brightest either. Kennedy, though, she has me. She will always have me. I'm not going anywhere.

"Thank you," I choke out. "Please call me if you find anything out," I tell her. I walk over and kiss her temple before grabbing my keys off the side.

"I'll drive," Harris shouts. I stop, turning around, not having time for this shit.

"Mine has Imogen's car seat," I yell back.

"You're also blocked in," he snaps and that's when I notice a car has pulled right up to my car, leaving me no room to pull out.

"Fuck," I growl, kicking the tyre of the offenders car. Fucking prick needs parking lessons.

FOURTEEN

EVAN

THE DRIVE OVER TO DAMON's mother's house feels like it's taking for fucking ever. With the weather as shit as it is, it isn't the main reason for slowing us down.

Every light we come across turns red, every crossing has had kids or other people crossing. Finally, we pull up to the country road leading to the mother's house. I'm literally bouncing in my seat ready to take this fucker down.

Taking a sharp bend the car skids to the side. Harris straightens the car but it's too late. The car ends up on the side of the road. He tries to reverse out, but the tyres skid, mud splattering the tyres. Putting the car into gear he tries to move forward but the car does the same.

We're fucking stuck.

"This is just fucking great," I shout, slamming my hands on the dashboard.

The backend wheels are spinning like crazy, mud flying all up the side of the car. Harris and I exchange looks before I jump out into the pouring rain, running around the back of the car.

"One, two, three," Harris shouts, revving the car. Mud splatters out from under the tyres and sprays all over me. So not only am I soaking wet but now I'm covered in fucking mud.

I push hard, the strength coming from all the pent up anger that I've been harbouring for the past couple of hours. I'm close. So fucking close to getting Imogen back and this happens.

My heart sputters to life when the car jerks forward, the movement nearly causing me to fly forward. I catch my footing before my face meets the ground and rush over, jumping back into the passenger seat.

My foot taps nervously on the car floor and I'm about ready to jump out when we pull up on her street. The tension in the car is suffocating, but I don't care, I just want my girl back.

"Slow down. If she's in there you don't want to go barging in and putting her in danger. Let's take a look around the back. Backup is on the way. They're five minutes out," Harris warns me. I know all the rules, all the guidelines, and have my own way of doing shit, but tonight? It's just gone to shit. The sky has completely darkened, the moon covered from the black clouds as the rain still falls heavily. It matches my mood perfectly.

There's a car lining the driveway when we pull up a few houses down. There are more on the street, but there's no telling if they're for the mother's house. When I take a look at the house the lights are shining brightly in every window.

"Well they're definitely in," I mutter.

"What do you want to do?" Harris asks looking around the rough neighbourhood.

"Hold on," I tell him, holding my hand up. I read the message on my phone, tapping out a quick reply before putting it back in my pocket. "Andrews is here. He's going to watch the front. We don't want to take a chance he'll escape."

"So we go around the back. C'mon."

We jump out of the car, walking up to the neighbour's driveway. I'm hoping the fucker is too wasted to be keeping a look out. I don't want him noticing us until it's too late. I don't want him to see it coming.

We slide around the back of the house to the back garden. The garden is fenced off so we jump over the fence into what has to be the dump. No, I'm fucking serious. Anything and everything fills the garden: shopping trolleys, fridge-freezers, sofas, an oven, and other rubbish and junk.

"The woman needs a trip to the tip," Harris mutters in disgust.

"I think this is the tip," I reply before moving slowly towards the backdoor.

We get closer to the backdoor; both of us crouched down under the kitchen window. Slowly sliding myself up the wall I go to take a look, but a baby's cry has me pausing in my tracks.

"Fuck," Harris whispers. Just then yelling begins in the house and my spine stiffens.

"Shut that fucking kid up," a woman yells over music and other voices.

"You shut her the fuck up. If I touch the thing I'm ripping it's lungs out," a man roars, earning laughter from whoever else is in the house. I don't stop to think. I'm up, leg raised and booting in the backdoor.

The first thing I see when I barge into the kitchen is that the room is filled with smoke. There are a few other guys standing around, but one look at my expression and they're backing out the kitchen door.

What happens next happens quickly. One minute Damon is standing across the kitchen table from me, then the next, he's jumping across it. Both of us charge at each other with full force and end up crashing into the table, the wood breaking around us.

"Where's my fucking daughter?" I yell, raising my fist to his face. His malicious grin fuels my rage and the red blood coating his teeth does nothing to satisfy my need to hurt him, to make him pay.

Punch after punch, I raise my fist, wanting to kill the fucker. All I see is red. I don't care about my job, about going to prison, or anything. I just want him to pay for what he's done.

"You're gonna fucking die," Damon roars spitting blood out at his feet.

A kick to my gut has me flying backwards and Damon is on me in a second. I block each blow like I'm trained, but it doesn't stop him from getting a few punches in.

More noise from the house reaches me but none of it registers. The only person I can see now is *him*, the only person in my mind is *him*, and I'm not going to stop until he's begging for mercy.

Kicking his legs out from under him gives me an advantage. I'm on him in a second and I grip him hard around the neck.

"I'm not the one dying tonight," I grit out, feeling my hands tighten their grip. His face begins to turn red, and I find satisfaction in that split second. Then he's gripping me around the waist with his legs, his arm grabbing my own neck and twisting us to the side. I land with a thud against a cupboard, a slight pain shooting in my side.

More shouting fills the kitchen along with the sound of glass smashing and other noises. I try to listen out for Imogen but Damon takes that split second of distraction to punch me in the ear, sending me off balance for a second.

Reaching up, I hit the palm of my hand as hard as I can into his nose. Blood spurts out all over the place and he howls in pain before kicking out at me again, connecting with my shins. His cries echo in my ears as I try to steady myself.

Fucking sissy.

I'm suddenly jumped from behind, my legs carrying me backwards from the sudden weight. Whoever the fuck is on me delivers a few punches to my head before I ram his back against the sink, his screams of agony howling across the kitchen. I throw him over my shoulder, hitting him at Damon who has just jumped to his feet, and knock them both to the floor. My breathing is erratic, sweat beading my forehead and body.

When Damon kicks the bloke away, I'm ready for him. I manage to deliver a few kicks to the ribs, before the wind is knocked out of me. In his hand Damon holds the thick, broken leg to the table, aiming at my side. My reflexes are becoming slow and he manages to knock me down to the floor.

He jumps up to his feet just as the sound of more voices fill the house. His startled eyes jump to me before jumping to the backdoor. I can see the decision in his eyes, and before he can make a run for it, I kick my feet out again, knocking him to the floor.

Lying on my back I lift my arms above me, the palms of my hands touching the floor before lifting my knees as close as I can to my head. Bending on my back a little I let my feet swing with power before swinging my upper body forward, the muscles in my stomach and back tightening. Once I'm vertical and standing on my feet steadily I move to the left, circling Damon. He doesn't hang around. As soon as the pads of his feet are touching the kitchen floor, he tries to move past me for the backdoor. He doesn't get far before I'm swinging my arm out, catching him in the chest. He grunts at the contact and I give him a smirk.

"Playing with fire, pig," he grits out. With a force I didn't think he had left in him, he has me by the shoulders and is hauling me across the kitchen, my body smacking hard into the kitchen sink. Cutlery crashes around me, plates and mugs smashing on the floor.

Rolling to the side, I roll off the kitchen sink and straighten up. Grunting I rush forward, swinging my fists into the side of his stomach. He hisses out a pain at the same time he lands another blow to my jaw, knocking me back a few steps. I soon gain composure and push him against the work bench on the other side of the kitchen, my hands gripping his neck in another tight squeeze. Only this time I show him no mercy.

Seeing his rugged scar across his face is just another reminder of how scared Kennedy was of him. Images of her bruised face and body flicker through my mind and it just causes my anger to rise.

"You'll fucking pay for what you've done to my woman and daughter," I growl. The metallic taste of blood invades my mouth and it's worse than the smell of blood filling the air in the tiny little kitchen.

"Fuck... you," he chokes out trying to spit at me.

I laugh throwing my head back and I know I sound manic. I'm crazy. I must be. I hear Harris shout something to me but the ringing in my ears hasn't stopped, it's blurred all of my senses of hearing, control, and reasoning.

When I look back down into the eyes of the soulless man that did this to my life, my world, I finally snap out of it. He needs to pay. And I don't mean paying from me ending his life. That's too easy for him. It'll only cause me to be punished for his wrongdoings. Going to jail because of a fucking loser like him isn't going to help me get Imogen back to her mother. It's not going to change what has happened and, as I said, it's too easy for him if I let him die.

I throw Damon off me, pushing his limp body back into the counter with a loud thud. Turning around I'm about to question Harris when I see something silver reflect in the kitchen light. It blinds me momentarily, enough time for me to notice Damon raise his hand.

Even exhausted, emotionally drained and only charged by my anger, I move quickly. My hand dashes out grabbing his wrist in a tight grip. I move forward, shovelling him backwards before taking his hand and slamming it up against the high wall cupboard. It takes me a few attempts before the knife drops to the floor. Once it's safe I move back and before he can take another swing at me, I rear my fist back, taking one last shot, knocking him out cold.

He falls to the floor in a heap and I don't bother moving to check if he's alright. I just turn to get my daughter.

Harris is there, his foot on a lady's back whilst he holds a screaming Imogen in his arms. She looks filthy. The fuckers haven't even bothered changing her. She's been lying in a shitty, wet nappy, the stench is nearly making me gag. It's soaked through her clothes, the stains are visible and my heart clenches.

She's still screaming her lungs out, her face is bright red, bordering on purple, but other than that, I can't see any cuts or bruises. That said, it still doesn't mean that there isn't some on her or that they haven't hurt her.

I keep my eyes locked with Harris' whilst grabbing Imogen from him. The second I get her in my arms I'm holding her tight in my arms. She cries harder, the sound breaking my heart. I check her over visually seeing no signs of any injuries which causes me to relax a little. But the smell of weed on her clothes has my body tightening all over again.

I need to know if the ambulance is on the way, so when I open my mouth to ask, a scuffle on the floor has me looking down. Harris has still got his foot pressed firmly down on who I presume is the mother. I end up giving him a strange look before my eyes rear back to the struggling woman on the floor.

"She resisted arrest," he shrugs and I can tell he's not telling me something when his eyes flick to the left.

"What did she do?" I bite out, wishing I could scrap my hitting no women policy just for a second. The woman is wearing dirty, grubby clothes that are far too big for her. I can see bone sticking out everywhere I look, and when my eyes reach hers they look just as cold and ragged as her expression.

"Look, the ambulance should be outside in a sec," he says, just as I hear the sirens moving closer. I move to the door just as he speaks. "Don't lose your head now. They're going to tell you eventually or you'll hear me inform the paramedic, but she had her hands wrapped round Immy's neck so make sure the paramedics look her over properly," he adds quickly, looking like he's ready to strain me if need be.

"Fuck." I'm torn on whether to hit a woman for the first time in my life, but having Imogen screaming in my arms reminds me she needs to get to the hospital. She needs to be checked over and she certainly needs to come before some dirty fucking scumbag. Damon's mom will pay for what she did, just like her son.

Walking out the door two officers come running up the front garden. "They're in the kitchen. One's knocked out, one is being restrained," I tell them as I walk straight to the ambulance. I'm about to walk into the back when the male paramedic stops me.

"Sorry, sir, but you'll have to wait. We have a patient that is unconscious that we need to deal with first," he says and I see red.

"No, you don't," I bite out. "You have a five month old baby that was kidnapped, strangled and filthy; she's covered in shit and piss. Now get in the front seat and drive us to the fucking hospital."

He opens his mouth and although he looks apologetic he seems like the type of guy who hates having his balls handed to him. He grunts under his breath.

"I'm going to call for another paramedic but I'll go check on him before I come back," the male paramedic tells us. I want to pull him back, tell him that fucker deserves to rot.

The female paramedic holds her arms out for Imogen and I hesitate for a second before handing her over. She's still squirming, her lungs protesting at her hoarse cries. When I found out about Imogen I knew I'd worry every second of every day. I'd be that dad that would be over protective, not letting her date and giving her a curfew. I'd be at every school play, every dance performance, and every sports day. But not once when I thought about our future did I consider feeling this kind of pain. Losing her never even registered in my head, I never prepared myself for it because it never felt like a possibility. I'd die before I let anything or anyone hurt her.

But today I failed.

I didn't protect her.

Now she's hurt, she's screaming and going through God knows what and there's nothing I can do.

Not even a week as her father and already I failed in the worst possible way.

"Can you tell us if she has any medical conditions?" the female paramedic asks gently, lying Immy down onto the bed.

My mind is blank. I know nothing. I know nothing about her medical conditions other than what Kennedy has told me about her birth. She hasn't said anything about any long lasting conditions.

Looking up at the paramedic, I scrub my hands down my face before answering her, giving her everything I know. "She was born an addict. I know she had some problems after being born, but I don't think it's on-going. I've only been in her life for a short while," I lie, not wanting to come across as a prick. I'm worried if I tell them I've only been in her life for a week that they won't let me stay with her.

"Are you the girl's father?"

"Yes," I nod watching her carefully for judgement, but when I see none I relax somewhat. It's obvious I'm involved in the law and the fact I've just announced Immy was born an addict, I can only imagine what they are thinking.

I reach out to Imogen and straight away she wraps her hand around my finger and I smile down at her, my heart splitting wide open.

"Can I change her?" the woman asks and I nod my head, feeling tears fill my eyes. I could have lost her. I could have lost her and her mother in the same day. I still don't know what's going on with Kennedy at the hospital, no one has got in touch with me since I left and I don't know whether that's good or bad. Just thinking about Kennedy all alone, hurting and suffering in that hospital has my heart beating faster and causes worry to form into the pit of my stomach.

I watch as she gently undresses her, using wet wipes to clean up her body. When she starts sticking pads to her chest I make a choking sound, my throat closing up.

"I need you to hold her arm for me?"

"What? Why?" I ask panicked.

"I need to get your daughter on an IV. She needs fluids," she explains as she messes around with her equipment.

Taking a huge breath I grab Immy's tiny arm in my hand, feeling sick to my stomach as she screams through the needle piercing her skin. The paramedic works quickly and fluently. When she's done she turns to the front of the ambulance.

I turn in the same direction noticing for the first time that the other paramedic has returned.

"We're good to go," she shouts through, grabbing a few other things off the side.

"Is she going to be okay?" I ask her once the car starts moving.

"I'm going to leave her unclothed for the time being and wrap her up warm in a blanket. Hopefully now that she's out of her soiled clothes and is getting some fluids inside her, she will be able to settle. She has some bruising on the side of her neck, finger marks clearly the cause. The doctors at the hospital will look over those when we arrive. Her heart rate is a little high at the moment but it's most likely due to stress her body is under. Once we have her settled and relaxed, we will be able to tell you more. There are no other clear signs of injury, but we have the best doctors waiting on standby in the ER."

"Thank you," I choke out, watching her move effortlessly tending to Imogen while the car moves steadily through traffic.

We're nearing the hospital when Imogen finally falls asleep from exhaustion, her tiny hand still gripping my finger with all its might.

The closer we get the harder I pray that when I walk into that hospital, Kennedy is awake and ready to greet us. We need her. Imogen needs her.

One way or another, I'm not leaving this hospital without both of my girls in my arms. In fact, once we're home, there is no way I'm ever letting them leave me again.

FIFTEEN

KENNEDY

Holy panthers, my head hurts. What is going on? What is that noise? I open my eyes with a struggle. They feel heavy like they're somehow glued together. Inside I'm panicking, wondering why I don't feel like I have control over my body. I lift my hand but that too feels heavy. My eyes water behind my eyelids. My tears seem to make it easier for me to open my eyes and when I do I'm taken aback when I find I'm lying in a hospital bed, tubes sticking from my arms and hands.

My head becomes too heavy to move anymore, and I look up at the dull, cream ceiling wondering why I'm here. What did I do? Loads of scenarios run through my head, but none are making any sense to me. My imagination is running wild with awful explanations but the headache pounding in my head is stopping anything real to form.

That's when the pain begins to register. At first it's just the pounding in my head, like someone has a hammer on the inside trying to smash their way out. My leg, chest, hell my whole body is throbbing in excruciating pain. Touching my hand to my head I feel a bandage wrapped around me and I begin to panic.

Needing to get up, I twist and turn in the bed, cries of pain leaving my mouth.

Even though my body is about to give up, I'm not. I need answers. Just when I'm about to open my mouth, to scream, the door opens to a girl I recognise walks through. She must hear the sound that escapes my mouth because her head snaps up and she gasps. She's looking at me with a mix of horror and concern.

In a panic I open my mouth to plead for answers. But in a blinding assault everything comes flooding back painfully.

Imogen.

Mel had called me. There was a break-in. Then Imogen was taken. Does anyone know? Has Mel called the police? Do they have her? Oh no! What if she's still out there and nobody knows? A strangled cry leaves my mouth.

I throw the covers off me, ignoring the pain that assaults my bruised, aching body. Any other time I'd feel ashamed, embarrassed, knowing *she* is seeing me at my most vulnerable. It's not a feeling I'm accustomed too. Especially with someone who dislikes me.

Sitting up feels like a chore, a painful, miserable chore. The gown they've dressed me in has an open back and I feel the breeze hitting my bare skin causing me to shiver. Nothing is going to stop me from getting to my daughter. Even if I have to wander these halls or the streets dressed in only this.

"Hey, Kennedy, it's me. Do you remember me? It's Denny, Evan's sister," the girl says sweetly and I look up to find tears in her eyes. Why is she crying? Has something happened to Imogen? Does she know something?

"You need... You need to help me. Imogen... I need to find Imogen," I cry. The pain in my throat feeling so raw, so painful, that it's beyond any sore throat I've suffered in the past.

"Calm down, Kennedy. Come on, get back into bed. You need to rest. I know about Imogen. Evan is going to get your daughter back, I promise," she says with conviction, her voice stern and full of promise.

"Why are you here?" I ask deflated. I do as I'm told, lying back down in bed. The look in her eyes leaves no room for argument and there's no way I have the strength to fight with her. Not when I need to save my strength for Imogen. She will need me.

"Lexi, Evan's next door neighbour, called me. She's outside. She didn't think you'd want her in here but she hasn't left. She's worried about you," Denny tells me. Lexi? Outside? And Denny is here. What the fudge have I woken up to. None of this feels real. Not Denny, not Lexi and not being in hospital.

"Is this real or am I dreaming?" I ask her seriously. She giggles just as the door opens.

"Is there any signs of her wake...Oh, hey, I'll wait outside," Lexi murmurs quietly, her face flushed.

"Lexi?" I call out, wondering what she's doing here. Does she know about Imogen or where Evan is?

"Hey," she calls back walking over to me slowly. She looks tired and worried and her concern shocks me after what she pulled with Evan. But I know if anyone has answers, she will.

"Where's Evan?" I ask, tears in my voice.

"He's gone to get your girl," she says giving me a small smile.

"He's found her?" I ask, my heart picking up hope.

"I'm not sure. When I left he was adamant she was at Damon's mother's house," she tells me honestly.

I gasp. My worry in the car about Damon had been right. That break-in was a set up, a trap to get my girl. But how did he know she'd be at Mel's? It's not like Mel and I go out and party together. All I know is, if she's with that monster she isn't safe.

His words repeat over and over in my head, the promise he made to sell Imogen and my vision becomes blurry.

I try to get up again knowing what Damon plans to do to her. He said he'd sell her. He only cares about getting his lousy three grand back. Three grand he willingly gave a drug addict in the first place. He doesn't care what my baby will be going through. That he's ruining her life or mine, that he's destroying two innocent people's lives.

"Hey, he'll find her. He loves you, Kennedy, he loves you both. He won't stop until he finds her," she tells me and I can hear the sincerity in her voice. She doesn't look sad by it, only sure of it.

"He's going to sell her," I cry out, the pain in my body becoming too much. Denny helps lay me back down, but my body remains stiff, and my tears remain to flow down my face.

"Who, Evan?" Denny asks confused.

"No. My sister was into some bad stuff. The man she owed money to came over to my house and beat me. He threatened to take Imogen and sell her."

"Oh, God," Denny cries, covering her mouth. "You've been going through so much. I didn't know. I'm so sorry for the way I acted. I was being stubborn and stupid. I never meant any of the things I said. None of it was even really about you. My stupid jealousy took over. I just miss my brother," she admits and I reach out and take her hand.

"It's fine. I understood where you were coming from. I just didn't want you to fight with each other because of me," I tell her, feeling my eyes water. "He loves you."

"I know. I just wish I dealt with everything that day a lot differently. Being a mom has changed me in so many ways, but I guess, deep down, I've still got that childishness in me. I've got a lot to learn," she admits sadly.

"You were being an overprotective sister," I smile, but it wobbles as more tears fall free. "I'm sorry too, for springing all that stuff on you without warning."

"Since we're all on the apology train, I want to say sorry too, Kennedy. What I did was uncalled for, but mostly, I'm sorry because I was in the wrong. I saw him happy and I suppose it got to me because I couldn't find *my* happy. Deep down I knew I'd never find it with him, but when I noticed he had it, I believed I could have that with him too. It was wrong of me. I'm just sorry I hurt you. You've done nothing but be kind to me, whereas, if I was you, I would have slammed the door in my face by now," she laughs, but it's forced, the smile not reaching her eyes.

I remember all the times she'd pass judgement when I would open the door. The look she would get in her eyes. Not once did I think she was jealous of the situation. I only saw her jealous of my relationship with Evan.

Knowing she got naked in front of Evan still angers me somewhat. But seeing Lexi now has me realising I've not really met the real her. She looks sincerely worried for my wellbeing and seems like a genuine person. Maybe if I hadn't come along she and Evan might have worked something out. The thought causes a sharp pain in my heart. Thinking of him with another woman makes me feel sick. But the thought he'd be better off without me has crossed my mind more than once since Lexi walked into the room.

"Please, don't. I can't handle anymore. Sometimes I think everyone would have been better off without me turning up," I cry, feeling sorry for myself. Imogen's life is ruined and Evan's will be destroyed if he doesn't get her back, and mine? Mine was doomed the second I got that call telling me that she was missing. The only reason Evan is even interested in me is because of Imogen. Without her there is no doubt he'd be with someone else right now. He would never look twice at a lowlife like me.

My feelings for Evan have grown over the week and with each day they have only grown stronger. Deep down I know if it wasn't for Imogen we wouldn't be together.

Denny must see the doubt written on my face because she tightens her hand around mine.

"No. Don't do that. I thought Mason was only with me because of Hope, but I was wrong. So fucking wrong," she sighs, smiling wistfully. "He loved me for me; Hope was just an added bonus. Evan loves you. He's never brought a girl home to meet us before... Ever. Not even at school. Don't let your head take you there, Kennedy. I might not know you, but from what Nan has said, you're the best thing since sliced bread," she giggles winking at me.

"Thank you," I croak out, before turning to Lexi. "And thank you. For coming here, and staying," I tell her, then a thought occurs to me. "How did you know I was here?" I ask Denny.

"Lexi called me. I had stayed at Evan's for a while last year and Lexi cleaned the house up before I arrived. She still had my number in her contacts. My nan is on her way too. She got stuck on some bridge. The river has overflowed or something, so she was waiting for everyone to turn back around before she could. She called twenty minutes ago telling me she was on her way."

"I don't deserve any of you," I tell her just as the door opens again.

A man I don't know walks in, followed by another who I know is Mason. No one could forget that face. He's still as handsome as when I first saw him. I remember Evan telling me he had four brothers, but looking to the man standing in front of him I know he isn't one of them. He has sandy blonde hair is messy and unkempt. He's larger than Mason but only by so much. He also carries himself with importance, a confidence you don't see in many people. He also has a lethal energy surrounding him. Something tells me you don't want to get on the wrong side of him. From the look on Lexi's face when he walks closer, I'd say she wouldn't care what side she got on. I have to stifle a giggle. I mean, how inappropriate would it be if I burst out laughing right now. My daughter is gone, Evan is gone, and I have no idea what the sugar is going on.

"Hey, I'm Aaron. I'm Evan's old partner?" the man in front introduces himself. I look up at him and nod, biting my lip. It must be the drugs they've got me on because I can't help the next thing that slips from my mouth.

"I didn't know he was gay," I mutter out loud. When I realise I've said it out loud, I begin to giggle. I giggle so hard that it begins to hurt my sides. My giggles turn into laughter, high, hysterical laughter.

One minute I'm laughing, laughing so hard that everything around me disappears. Then they become sobs. The first one that breaks is painful and it echoes around the now silent hospital cubical.

Denny takes me in her arms, letting me sob into her chest. "I need her back," I cry, my emotions all over the place. I try to get myself together. Being in this state is not going to help anyone.

"I meant work partner," I hear Aaron mutter before hearing Lexi giggle.

"Where is he?" I ask turning my head, still sniffling. I don't move, keeping myself locked in Denny's arms, needing her comfort.

Mason walks around the bed looking between us and when he looks back up to Denny, his eyes go soft.

That's so sweet, I think when he reaches her, leaning over to kiss her forehead. If only I had Evan here. Even better, Imogen. My heart is breaking having neither here with me. I need them. I'll always need them.

"He's downstairs getting Imogen checked over," Aaron states and I must not have heard him right, so I sit up better, wincing when the pain becomes too much. My leg hurts the most. I only have to turn my head and a pain radiates down my leg, all the way down to my toes.

"I'm sorry, but could you repeat that, slowly," I tell him, looking at his mouth, making sure I don't miss a word.

"He's downstairs getting Imogen checked over," he says and his lips twitch looking at my immobile state.

"Oh my gosh," I cry out, my hands flying to my mouth. "Is she okay? Where was she? Is she hurt? Is she going to be okay? Tell me?" I yell at him, feeling hysterical, causing a nurse to come running in.

"What's going on in here?" she asks sternly, eyeing the men in the room warily.

"We're good," Aaron tells her winking before turning back to me. "She's fine. She just needs to wait for the doctor to give her the okay to leave before he can come up. He wants to come up and see you but he doesn't want to leave Imogen. I offered to watch over her but he nearly knocked me out," he teases.

The nurse walks over and starts checking the machines out. I think I'm in shock because there's nothing I can say. She's been found. She's safe. She's okay. Evan is safe. My heart beats rapidly and the machine next to me starts beeping like mad. The nurse walks over and says something, but my mind is on one thing.

My daughter.

My daughter is safe.

"Miss, I need you to calm down."

"She's safe. She's safe," I cry and Denny hugs me. I sob into her shoulder just as the door opens again.

Expecting it to be another nurse or maybe a doctor, I pull back. But when a large form looms in the doorway, my breath is taken away.

"Evan," I breathe out, and everything I was feeling seconds ago starts to simmer away.

SIXTEEN

EVAN

THE DOCTORS FINALLY GIVE Imogen the all clear.

"Just keep a close eye on her. If anything changes, don't hesitate to call the number on the leaflet I gave you," the doctor tells me.

"Are you sure she's okay?" I ask again. If there's a chance she's not going to be okay then why aren't they making her stay in for observation?

"Yes. Her blood pressure is back to normal and she's hydrated. There is no swelling inside her throat but the swelling around her bruises will take a few days to go. You can take your daughter home, Mr. Smith."

I nod, holding a sleeping Immy in my arms. After being here for a few hours I'm finally able to check on my woman. No one has been able to give me any new information. All they've said is she's stable but still unconscious.

Like that makes me feel any better.

Aaron came down not long ago to keep me updated. He offered to watch over Immy while she was sleeping but the look in my eyes must of told him that wasn't going to happen. I feel like I've had to choose between the woman I love, and the girl I love, and I've hated every second of it. I even asked at one point if they could treat Immy upstairs where her mom was, but they told me no.

Assholes.

We're walking down the corridor when I hear footsteps rushing toward us from behind.

"Oh good Lord, there you are. My little girl," my nan cries and I look around wondering where the fuck she came from. The hallway was clear when we rounded the corner. She must have been running fast to catch up to us that quickly.

"Hey, Nan," I greet, feeling drained. I'm worried sick about Kennedy and I'm still not sure I should have let them discharge Immy. No matter how sincere the doctor looked when she spoke to me.

We're on the floor Kennedy is on now which is a different ward than the one she was on earlier. When I stop walking to greet my nan, she holds her hands up for Immy, but I just hold her tighter to my chest. She's still wrapped up in a blanket but thankfully she now has a nappy on thanks to one of the nurses.

I remembered Lexi packing clothes for both of the girls. I just hope it was something warm because I don't want my girl being cold. She's suffered enough today as it is.

"Oh, come on, Evan. I've been stuck in bloody traffic feeling sick with worry about my two girls. Let me hold her."

"I'm sorry, Nan, and I mean no harm when I say this, but I'm not letting her go. The next time she's out of my arms will only be to place her rightfully in her mother's," I tell her and her eyes go gentle a fraction more before she bursts into tears.

"You're such a good boy, Evan. Come on. Let's go see how my daughter-in-law is doing," she smiles. "Have you heard anything yet?" she asks, but my mind is still focused on 'daughter-in-law'.

"What?" I ask astonished, my eyes snapping to hers with awe. How the hell does she know I plan on asking Kennedy to marry me? Not that I'm giving Kennedy much of a choice. After today I know I won't be able to live without her or Imogen. There's no way I'm letting them go.

"Oh calm your horses, my boy. I saw the way you looked at her when I came to meet her. But back then you didn't have wedding bells shining in your eyes. Now you do," she tells me. I give her a shrug, not bothering to deny it. I will be marrying her even if she refuses. I'll drag her skinny, fine ass down that aisle kicking and screaming.

We reach the door to Kennedy's room and I instantly hear voices coming from inside before loud sobs echo through the hall. Her cries hit my chest with a sharp pain and I have to compose myself before pushing the door open. Kennedy is crying into my sister's chest. The picture shocks me. When I prepared myself to walk into this room I pictured walking inside to find her alone. I can't believe she's here, consoling my girl of all people. Mason is next to Denny looking uncomfortable and I would laugh if it wasn't for the fact my girl was now looking at me like she has seen a ghost.

"Evan," she gasps.

"Hey, babe," I smile and walk over. Lexi and Aaron move out of the way, Aaron putting his arm around her as they move towards the window.

She bursts into tears again, her eyes locked on mine, and her hand reaching for Immy.

"You've got fractured ribs, baby. Be careful," I warn her and my sister moves out of the way but doesn't move far. I look up and give her a thankful smile. I'm guessing Aaron called her.

"Lexi called me," she whispers, reading my mind. She looks back down to Kennedy who is now holding a sleeping Immy in her arms while sobbing. Denny's eyes soften, her eyes watering as she looks down at Kennedy in understanding, the only way another mother could understand.

Looking back at Kennedy, checking her over to see if she's okay, I can tell it's paining her to hold Immy, but I also know she'd walk on fire to be with her.

I turn my head to Lexi and mouth 'thank you' before stroking my girl's face, the part that isn't messed up with cuts and bruises.

"How are you feeling?" I rasp out, overjoyed to see my girls back together.

"So much better now that you're both here where you belong," she tells me, giving me a watery smile. I lean down kissing the top of her head. "Is she okay? What happened?"

"She's fine. They've checked her over and given her the all clear."

"She's bruised," she chokes out, tears still rolling down her face as she lightly strokes Immy's hand where the IV had been put in.

"Yeah, baby," I tell her, not knowing what else to say. "The paramedics had to link her up to an IV," I start, but pause not knowing how to tell her about the bruises on Imogen's neck. Kennedy's hand reaches out to squeeze mine and I give her a small smile.

"What happened?"

"She was taken by Damon. We found her at his mom's house. They've both been arrested and won't get off on the charges. There's too many against them."

"Is that why you're covered in bruises and have a fat lip?" she asks, not taking her eyes from Immy.

"Yeah," I chuckle and when she moves the blanket she notices the bruises on Immy's neck. She gasps, looking at me horrified.

"What happened? Oh my gosh, why have they let her out? Is she okay? Are you sure?" she cries, lightly rubbing over the bruises.

"Yeah, she's a fighter. I made sure to get another doctor to double check her injuries. I think towards the end they wanted to sedate me," I chuckle, trying to ease the mood.

Everyone listens intently in the room but I ignore them, my main focus entirely on my two girls.

"Why is she naked?" she asks concerned, her nose scrunching up.

"She was dirty from not having her nappy changed, baby. Let's not worry about it now. She's safe, back with us where she belongs. They can't hurt us anymore, okay?"

She smiles, but it doesn't reach her eyes and I can see the concern shining in her eyes for her daughter. I lean in giving her another kiss when the nurse speaks up. I hadn't even noticed her in the room.

"I'm sorry but visiting hours are over. I know about your situation so I spoke to the ward nurse and she said it was fine to have two people stay. But I'm afraid I'll have to ask the rest of you to go," she tells us sadly.

We nod our heads, Aaron, Lexi, Mason and Denny saying they'll leave us to it. Needing to have a word with my family a second, I look down to Kennedy before speaking. "Let me go talk to them outside, and then I'll be back. Nan, can you stay here for a second and watch over them?"

"Of course," she says, waving me off from the end of the bed.

Denny leans over whispering something to Kennedy before hugging her gently. Mason moves and the poor kid doesn't even know how to address her. He ends with just patting her shoulder a few times before leaning in and kissing her cheek. I'm not going to lie, sister's boyfriend or not, I want to smack his face away from hers.

Denny must have noticed my expression because she starts to giggle. Taking

Mason's hand she steps back before walking out the room, leaving everyone else to say their goodbyes. I follow behind them hearing Lexi saying goodbye along with Aaron, before they too, follow us out.

When we're all outside I turn to Lexi first. Her eyes widen when she feels my attention on her. Before she can open her mouth I move forward quickly, pulling her against me for a tight hug. I know she's not expecting it when I feel her body tighten, but I need her to know how thankful I am. How happy I am that she put everything going on aside and was a friend to me. The friend that I've missed the past few months. Without her help today, Kennedy would be lying in that room on her own, scared out of her mind with worry. For that, I'll be forever thankful.

"I'm so fucking thankful to you, Lexi. For everything," I whisper hoarsely. "It kills me knowing that she was on her own. You knew that and came. Even after everything," I rasp out.

"Don't worry about it," she tells me, playing it off. I give her another squeeze before pulling away. She looks up at me with a sad smile. "I hope everything is going to be okay with you all. I'm only next door if you need anything, ever. I'm so sorry for the way I've been acting. I haven't been myself and I'm so embarrassed."

"Let's not worry about any of that anymore. Fresh start?" I ask, giving her a genuine smile.

"Yes. I'd like that. Oh, and the bags of stuff I brought with me for Imogen and Kennedy are in the cabinets beside the bed. The nurse said to leave them there. If I had known you were in the hospital sooner I would have brought them to you and Imogen."

I nod. "Thank you. For everything."

"Call me if you need anything," she tells me.

"Promise," I smile, leaning in and kissing her temple. She smiles up at me before moving to the side.

Aaron steps forward next, patting me on the shoulder. "You need more time at the gym, mate. He really did a number on you," he teases, but I notice the way his eyes darken.

"You haven't seen the other fucker," I chuckle.

"Let's hope you did a good number on him," he winks, before giving me the head nod. You know the one that says, 'I'm glad your missus and kid are okay.'

He walks off and his words play around in my head. Damon really did do a number on me. In more ways than one. But one thing he didn't get to do is break me. All I have to do now is make sure he didn't break my woman. But no matter the answer to that, I'll make sure I spend the rest of my life putting her back together.

I watch as he takes Lexi's arm before walking down the corridor. Seeing them together is another reminder that I need to set the two up. If they haven't already hooked up, that is. This isn't the first time I've seen them together that the same exact thought hasn't occurred to me.

Turning my body I face my sister. Guilt and shame hit me when I look at her tear streaked face.

"I'm sorry," I tell Denny at the same time she says, "I'm really sorry." We both start launching at each other before turning serious. Not waiting, I wrap her tightly in my arms, squeezing the life out of her. I've missed her so fucking much. It feels like I've distanced myself from her since I moved out. One of the reasons I did was because of our 'mom'. I felt guilty leaving her there knowing what a monster our mother was. It wasn't until the kidnapping, knowing our mother's part in it, that I truly felt ashamed. I'd been so focused on my job, on moving forward, that I didn't reach out to her often. I'm just glad we have this second chance.

"Thank you for coming," I tell her through the dryness in my throat. It must have taken her a lot to come here with how she feels about Kennedy. "I know how you feel about Kennedy, but you still came," I begin.

"She's family," she says stopping me. "I was being selfish and childish and should never have reacted the way I did. It was uncharacteristic. I've told Kennedy I'm sorry and I am. But I'm also sorry to you. The way I behaved," she says shaking her head as if she's remembering her behaviour.

"It's fine. It's over now. I'm just fucking glad you're here," I choke out before grabbing her into another hug.

She chuckles in my ear before whispering, "Take care of them."

"I will, forever," I smile, kissing her cheek and pulling back.

"We're staying in a hotel not far from here. The bridge is all flooded and the roads are still bad. I don't want to risk us getting in a crash," she tells me, and I start to feel bad that she has to spend the night away from Hope. I know it must be hard for her. It would kill me to spend a night away from Immy now that I've got her in my life. I can now understand why my sister fought so fiercely to keep Hope. I'd do the exact same thing for Imogen.

"Go get some rest. I'll speak to you tomorrow," I smile, ready to get back inside to Kennedy and Immy.

I watch her walk down the corridor in Mason's arms. It's then I realise how lucky I am to have the sister I do. She could be annoying like other sisters that I know about through mates, but she's not. She's anything but. She's always been understanding and older than her years. She has clawed her way through some tough times and I truly admire her for it.

When they're no longer in sight I turn back to the door that holds my future.

Walking into the room, Nan has found the bag of clothes that Lexi packed and is currently in the middle of singing to Immy while changing her at the end of Kennedy's bed. None of them hear me walking in so I take the time to take in everything. How my life became this in such a short amount of time is crazy, but one thing is for certain, I wouldn't change anything for the world.

The door opens behind me snapping me out of my thoughts. Nan and Kennedy startle at the sound and at seeing me already standing there. I smile sheepishly before moving out of the nurse's way. She walks in carrying a bottle and pushing a crib and I smile.

"I pinched this from the maternity ward. Imogen is fine to stay here with you and your fiancé," the nurse smiles and I look to Kennedy, worried about how she'll react at hearing me being called fiancé. She's about to open her mouth to tell the nurse that we're not getting married, I can see it. So before she can get anything out I rudely interrupt.

"Thank you. That's really kind and understanding of you. We appreciate it, don't we, babe?" I say before moving over towards Kennedy. She's watching me open mouthed, but there's no denying the spark in her eyes at hearing her being called my fiancé. It makes me really fucking pleased to see she's not disgusted by it.

Taking a seat in the chair next to the bed, I pull it as close as I can towards Kennedy as it will go, taking her hand in mine. When Nan walks around the bed and hands me a dressed Immy, I smile. She's fully awake now and her big blue eyes are staring up at me.

"I've got to go check in to a hotel. The radio has been giving out flood warnings all day so I don't think I'll drive back tonight. I'm going to book in then get some food. Would you two like me to bring something in for you? The hospital food isn't that great. My friend Doris had her gallbladder out not long ago here, and said the food was enough to put someone in the hospital," she tuts, sounding disgusted with the food.

"Please," I smile, thankful she thought about it. I ignore her comment about hospital food, not wanting to listen to her get into another one of her rants. Instead, I grab the bottle the nurse left placed on Kennedy's lap and start feeding Immy.

Now washed and dressed in clean clothes Immy is happier. She gulps her bottle down like she hasn't been fed, but then I grit my teeth when I realise she hasn't. The only source of food she's had is whatever she had at Mel's, and the IV she got put on. She could have starved to death.

Fuck! We really could have lost her today. The thought guts me.

The door shuts behind the nurse and I look up to Kennedy wondering if she's gone to sleep. She's been really quiet since I walked back into the room and I wonder if she blames me for everything, but instead, I find her watching me with a look I can't decipher.

"Why do they think I'm your fiancé?" she asks quietly. A pink blush rises on her cheeks and she looks away for a split second before her eyes reach mine again.

"Because you are, baby. You don't have a choice in the matter - it would be hugely appreciated if you would agree, and as soon as you're well enough, we're getting married."

"We are?" she breathes and her eyes start to water.

"Yeah, baby. We are," I tell her softer this time, letting her see how fucking honest I'm being right now. I want her to belong to me in every possible way.

"But... But we've not known each other that long," she tells me, trying to protest. Her words hold no heat behind them so I know she wants this as much as I do.

"Baby, I knew the day I met you I was going to marry you. It just took me until today to realise that."

"I love you," she rasps out, a sob breaking free as she tries to give me a small smile.

"I love you too, baby. Now get some rest. We've got forever."

EPILOGUE

KENNEDY

Here's a sneak peek of what's to come in Max's novel, book four in the Carter Brother Series, but in Kennedy's POV.

WHAT THE FUDGE IS THAT god awful sound? My ears are ringing, or it could be a phone, I'm not sure.

What I do know is, I'm never drinking again. Ever! And I mean never, ever. I hate alcohol and as of today I'm never drinking the stuff again or even socialising with the stuff. Alcohol and I are not friends, at all.

Last night is a complete blur. Little parts come to mind, but nothing that explains why I feel like I'm dying. I feel like I've been hit by a truck all over again.

"Babe, you're going to wake Immy up with your groaning," my husband chuckles, and I bury my head further into the pillow. And yes, I said husband.

Evan kept to his word and as soon as I was better he hauled me to a register office where we got married. I've still got my cast on in my wedding photos, but I don't care. The only thing that mattered to me that day was marrying Evan. We also got his name on Imogen's birth certificate and managed to get her last name changed.

Everything is perfect.

I've never been in love with someone as much as I am with him.

But right now I want to kick him out of bed. I'm actually kind of missing my cast, I could use it right about now to kick him out.

"Stop talking," I grumble, pouting into the pillow.

"Babe," he chuckles, shaking my shoulders. The notion causes a wave of nausea to assault my stomach and I growl.

After everything was sorted between me and Denny, and Evan and Denny, she became a new fixture in my life. She's declared me her sister, but the way I'm feeling this morning, she's no sister of mine.

It was Denny's hen party last night, hence the reason for my major hangover. Evan had skipped going to the bucks night because he didn't want anyone else watching Imogen.

Even though neither of us blame Melanie for Imogen being taken, we've both agreed to watch over her ourselves. It's only until the memory of what happened to Immy isn't so fresh in our minds and we're comfortable leaving her with someone else. Melanie feels remorse for what happened, but agrees she couldn't handle watching over her again. What happened scared her more than we realised. She's getting better now but still after eight weeks, I had hoped she'd visit us more or let us visit her.

The ringing starts back up and I grunt into the pillow, wishing the noise would stop.

"Babe, it's Denny. She's called a thousand times already this morning."

Moving my head I wince at the light in the room and narrow my eyes on Evan as he hands me the phone. He chuckles, kissing my forehead.

"I'll get you a coffee," he whispers before moving off the bed. I watch distractedly as he walks away, his tight buns tensing in his boxers.

Fudging hell, my husband is hot.

"We're not friends anymore," I grumble into the phone, feeling the room spinning around me still.

Denny screams down the phone and I pull the phone away from my ear, wincing at the ear splitting sound. "Calm down and stop the shouting," I yell, but wince at the pain shooting in my skull.

"I need your help, or someone's help. I think I cheated on Mason," she cries.

At first my mind is shocked that she'd cheat on him, but then I vaguely remember her being carried off somewhere by Mason himself.

"No you haven't. He brought you home, didn't he?"

"I don't know. He's not here. I'm walking over to Joan's now. I can't believe I've cheated on him. I'd never do this. I can't even remember last night. What the hell happened? Why did I wake up wearing half of a leather hooker's outfit, and how the hell did I get a fucking tattoo." she cries hysterically.

I moan down the phone, not remembering a thing. Everytime an image pops into my mind it's blurry. I don't know what's real and what's not.

"You got a tattoo?" I croak, my voice dry and hoarse.

"Yes, it's actually really awesome, but that's not the point. I don't remember getting the fucking thing. Please, what did we do last night?"

"I honestly don't know, Denny. I remember dares," I tell her and I can't help but giggle at her hooker statement. "You've really got on a hooker outfit?"

"Kennedy, it's not funny," she cries. "I'm wearing leather. Fucking leather. I'm a mother for Christ's sake. What the hell did we do? Hold on, I got a message."

I hear her pressing buttons on her phone before she bursts out laughing.

"Oh my God. You're never going to believe this," she laughs.

"What?" I ask, wondering what could be worse than getting a tattoo and waking up wearing leather.

"Max..." she laughs, struggling to breathe. "He's been arrested... Again. He was found jaywalking naked from Hawthorn Farm," she laughs and I begin to laugh with her.

What the hell did we do last night?

Find out what they get up to in Max's novel, book four in the series.
Release date TBA

OTHER TITLES BY LISA HELEN GRAY

If you enjoyed, Evan's story make sure you check out
the other books in the Carter Brother series.

AUTHORS NOTE

I never intended to write Evan's book. When I first began planning the Carter Brother series, Evan never even crossed my mind.

Then I released Mason and I had so many people asking me if Evan was getting his own book. It got me thinking straight away. We already discovered there was something between Evan and his next door neighbour Lexi, but I wanted something more for him.

In came Kennedy.

She came to me in a dream and I loved her character so much I decided to give her to Evan.

After that the whole story pretty much came together by itself.

I didn't want to write a full novel for Evan due to the fact that this is a Carter Brother series, so I ended up going for a novella.

I honestly hope my readers enjoy his book, and are looking forward to reading Max's. These characters have become such a huge part of my life that I feel like I live with them sometimes. Even my kids ask me what I have planned for them.

I want to thank everyone who has supported me, who helped me put this book together. Charlotte for sticking by me, and always listening to everything I have to say.

I want to thank my beta team for always reading and giving me back some fantastic pointers. You guys have been with me pretty much from the start, and are as much a part of this journey as anyone. You ladies rock!

And thank you to my newest part of the team, Elisia Goodman. She literally saved my ass on more than one occasion since I hired her in December. She worked around the clock to help me get Myles and Evan finished in time. We had some sets back but everyone has been really understanding.

Then to my fellow readers....

I don't even know where to begin. One minute I was writing for fun, getting all these stories down for my own benefit, then the next, I'm self-published and have so many followers I don't even know what to do with myself.

Many authors will agree, and say they never expected to get this far, but hand on heart, I honestly didn't think I'd sell ten books let alone the amount that I do. It's been so overwhelming that at times none of it feels real. I'll have readers email me, telling me that I've made them cry, that they love my work and can't wait for the next book in the series to be released. I try my best to reply to everyone who writes to me, and to acknowledge everyone who writes a review, good or bad. For you to take that time out of your lives, to write little old me a review, is amazing. It's surreal.

So thank you. You've made my dream come true and you continue to let it come true with every book of mine that your pick up and read. It means everything to me.

ABOUT LISA

Lisa Helen Gray is Amazon's bestselling author of the Forgotten Series and Carter Brother series.

She loves hanging out, but most of all, curling up with a good book or watching movies. When she's not being a mom, she's been a writer and a blogger.

She loves writing romance novels, ones with a HEA and has a thing for alpha males.

I mean, who doesn't!

Just an ordinary girl surround by extraordinary books.

Printed in Great Britain
by Amazon

81409217R00075